Finding a Sacred Oasis in Illness

Pastoral Care Package
Volume I

A Resource Manual for
Clergy and Lay Visitation

Department of Spiritual Wellness
Shawnee Mission Medical Center
Shawnee Mission, Kansas

By
Steven L. Jeffers, PhD
Community Outreach Project Coordinator

©2001

ISBN: 1-58597-076-X

Library of Congress Control Number: 2001088461

Finding a Sacred Oasis in Illness
Pastoral Care Package, Volume I
© 2001 Shawnee Mission Medical Center Foundation
All rights reserved, including the right
to reproduce this book or portions thereof in any form.

For information contact:
Steven L. Jeffers at
Shawnee Mission Medical Center
9100 W. 74th Street
Shawnee Mission, KS 66204
(913) 676-2305

Foreword

There has been an increased interest in the role spirituality plays in health. Data suggests that patients want their spiritual issues addressed, and for some patients spiritual beliefs play a major role in how they cope with stress and with suffering. Victor Frankl in his experience in a concentration camp concluded that *"Man is not destroyed by suffering but he is destroyed by suffering without meaning."* Spiritual and religious beliefs help people find meaning in the midst of pain and suffering.

As people face a serious and perhaps life-threatening illness, lots of questions often arise. Questions like "why me, why now, what will my future hold?" People often begin to question the very purpose and meaning of life. Some people question God's existence and others simply question the fairness of life and the reason for suffering. These questions might lead people down a spiritual path.

In today's healthcare system, people can get lost in technology and the focus on physical healing or cures. The spiritual questions often get ignored and not supported. However, increasingly, physicians and other healthcare providers have come to recognize the need to focus not only on the physical but also on the social, emotional, and spiritual issues patients face. Physicians, nurses and others are being trained to do spiritual histories. Integral to their training is the recognition of and the referral to chaplains and other spiritual care providers. The Joint Commission on Accreditation of Health Care Organizations (JCAHO) has written that:

> *"Pastoral counseling and other spiritual services are often integral to the patient's daily life. When requested the hospital provides or provides for pastoral counseling services."*

I feel strongly that chaplains and lay spiritual care providers should be integral members of the healthcare teams. As our patients struggle with spiritual questions in the midst of their illness, it is crucial that we provide the support and attention to our patient's spiritual needs. Our patients need companions on their spiritual path. This resource manual provides the needed information to help clergy and lay spiritual care providers give patients the needed spiritual support to help them heal.

Christina M. Puchalski, MD
Assistant Professor,
George Washington University
School of Medicine;
Director of Education,
National Institute for Healthcare Research
Department of Medicine

My Prayer for You
By: Steven L. Jeffers

I asked my God to bless you
When I talked to Him today,
To encourage and support you
As you journey along life's way.

He is always present with you;
He is ever faithful and true.
In no way will He forsake you;
He promises to be there for you.

So if a path you might travel
Is more troublesome than the rest,
Ask God in His love to show you
What is His very best.

Authority and Mandate for Visitation

"... By what kind of authority are you doing these things? Or who gave to you this authority in order that you may do these things?"

You have a three-fold source of authority to visit the sick and shut-ins.

- ❖ **Authority from God**

- ❖ **Authority from Institutions (e.g. church, hospital, nursing home)**

- ❖ **Authority from patient / resident**

"Is anyone suffering misfortune or hardship among you, let him pray; Is anyone encouraged, let him sing a hymn of praise; Is anyone sick or ill among you, let him call forth the elders of the church and let them pray over him after anointing him with oil in the name of the Lord. And the vow/prayer from faith shall heal the sick and discouraged... The earnest, operative petition of a righteous person has much power."

Introduction

A primary function of the professional clergy person and lay minister is to care for others. According to Martin E. Marty in the book *Hospital Ministry*, the phrase "care for" has a double meaning. On the one hand, it can mean, "has an appreciation of." Thus, virtually every hospital patient who seeks spiritual things as a part of the overall healing does "appreciate" the clergy person or lay volunteer. On the other hand, "care for" can mean, "take care of." This latter understanding of "care for" prescribes that the professional/lay minister move beyond simply being appreciated and adopt the role of παρακλητός (parakletos), a word which literally translates as "one called along side," but is most often rendered as "helper" or "comforter." "Care for" rendered in this fashion and appropriated in ministry to the hospitalized and shut-in is, in the truest sense, "taking care of" those who are suffering and making them acutely aware of the fact that disease need not and should not touch the soul.

This concept of "care for" is eloquently articulated by ethicist Daniel Callahan of The Hastings Center when he explains the need to face "the psycho-social-spiritual dynamics of caring."

> *It is the suffering of illness, not simply the pain it may bring, that most oppresses: our fears about the future, our feeling of loss, our anxiety that control and self-direction are, or may be, no more.*
>
> *To care for another is to minister to these fears, to supply love and patient fidelity to the anxiety about separation from others. It is to assure that they remain important to others, that the illness has not deprived them of a life in the community. It is to ease their pain where possible, and then help them live with their frailty, whether of body, mind or function."*

Furthermore, according to Harold Koenig, M.D., in *The Healing Power of Faith:*

> *"Healing can include dramatic, sudden physical cures, but is not confined to the 'miraculous' or spectacular. Perhaps for most people, the healing power of faith involves a healing of the mind and emotions, of the intangible spirit, and of relationships with others. In the end, achieving this type of inner peace may or may not result in physical healing; but even if the physical is not healed, it is very likely the burden of illness may be lighter... Healing faith often involves persistence and patience, a kind of positive thinking. This type of faith can put physical illness beneath us, where it belongs, return dominion to us, and give us power to live victorious and fulfilled lives."*

You as a representative of God communicate this healing power of faith to those you visit.

Therefore, based upon the previous discussion, I do not think there is any doubt that a ministerial presence with the hospitalized and shut-in is not only appreciated, but an absolute essential to facilitate holistic healing. Having said that, hospital and nursing home visitation of the sick and shut-in is a mandate, not an option. The hospital/nursing home and patient/resident need and welcome the ministry you provide.

> *"Every action, under certain circumstances and for certain people, may be a stepping stone to spiritual growth...."*
>
> Christopher Isherwood

To aid that valuable ministry is the purpose for which this manual was prepared. The people to whom you minister deserve a qualitative ministry. And so, in an attempt to sharpen your own skills and those of your lay ministers, we have researched and included materials from hospital chaplains, professors of pastoral care, and other professional caregivers to that end. Take what is helpful and incorporate it into your own style of ministry.

Lastly, I would encourage you to be open to the strong possibility that you might be blessed as a result of your visit with the sick. I can remember many occasions when that very thing happened to me: I, the minister, was the one who received ministry from the one to whom I intended to impart ministry. Hospital visits can, and perhaps should, be dual blessings: to the one who visits and to the one who is visited.

Respectfully,

Steven L. Jeffers, PhD
Community Outreach Project Coordinator
Department of Spiritual Wellness
Shawnee Mission Medical Center

Acknowledgments

I would be remiss not to publicly and profoundly thank the many people who contributed so much toward the completion of this resource manual. These contributions came in different forms: submission of materials for insertion into the text, review of the text, and typing the text.

Of these several people who provided materials for this project, my utmost appreciation is for a dear friend and former teaching colleague, Dr. J. Thomas Meigs, Minister of Pastoral Care and Wellness of Park Cities Baptist Church, Dallas, Texas. To a large degree, Dr. Meigs provided the inspiration for the writing of this manual by sharing with me some material he had prepared to train deacons in his congregation for hospital ministry. Additionally, he graciously gave his permission for me to use whatever of that material I deemed appropriate in this manual. Therefore, as a tribute to Dr. Meigs, some of the material contained in this manual, although adapted, is derived from the one he compiled.

I also want to thank a number of my colleagues in the Saint Luke's-Shawnee Mission Health System for their helpful comments and suggestions. They are: Mark Fenton and retired CPE Program Supervisor Dr. Robert Carlson; Nursing Supervisor, Rose Mary Sanders and nurses on her staff, along with nurses from other areas of the hospital. Moreover, I am very appreciative of Administrative Director Ivan Bartolome's and Spiritual Wellness Department Manager Jerry Rexin's careful and thoughtful work with the manuscript. Mr. Bartolome also did an outstanding job in graphics design for which I am truly grateful.

Furthermore, Quentin Jones, Senior Pastor of Merriam Christian Church, and Dr. Harold Ivan Smith, a prolific author and popular speaker on grief, were very instrumental in providing comments and suggestions which enhance the quality and relevance of content for a resource manual of this nature. No project like this, though, could be brought to fruition without an accomplished editor like Martha Rexin. Thanks, Martha!

Moreover, I am grateful to Jim Boyle, Sam Turner, Robin Harrold, Sheri Hawkins, and Keith Richardson, senior administrators of Shawnee Mission Medical Center, for their valuable contributions to the success of this endeavor. Similarly, appreciation is extended to Bill Grosz and Lou Gehring, executives of Shawnee Mission Medical Center Foundation, for their unwavering confirmation of the importance of such a book. In addition, I am thankful for Bob Woolford's work of advocacy of this book's value to other hospitals throughout the United States.

Finally, I am deeply indebted to Bill Robertson, former CEO of Shawnee Mission Medical Center, and Jerry Rexin, whom I previously mentioned, for their encouragement and support for this project.

Steven L. Jeffers

Table of Contents

Foreword iii
My Prayer for You v
Authority and Mandate for Visitation vi
Introduction vii
Acknowledgments x

Life in a Hospital: A Patient's Perspective
   What Is a Hospital? 1
   What Is a Hospital Patient? 4
   What Is It Like To Be Hospitalized? 11
   The Attachment of Meaning and Purpose to Illness 14
   Patient's Needs – Another Viewpoint 16

Insights of and Strategies for Pastoral Care in a Hospital Setting
   Pastoral Care: A Noble Ministry with a Rich Tradition 18
   The ABC's of Hospital Visitation 23
   Nuances of Nursing Home Ministry 26
   Visiting the Sick or Shut-In: A Checklist of Things To Consider 28
   Practical Suggestions for Hospital Visitation 32
   Nurses Speak Out 34
   Perspectives on Ministry of Presence 37
   Importance of the Ministry of Presence 39
   Additional Thoughts on the Ministry of Presence 40
   Humor: A Good Medicine for Suffering 42
   Medicate the Patient 46
   A Sample Prescription Form 53
   A Decalogue for Those Who Care for the Seriously Ill 58
   Ministry Needs for the Seriously Ill: A Patient's Perspective 60
   Hope: A Timeless Treasure 65
   Hope-Inspiring Strategies 68
   Talking with Sick People 69
   Listening: A Balm for Healing 72
   More Tips on Listening as a
      Vital Component of Effective Ministry 75
   A Case Study in Effective Listening 82

Prayer: An Essential Element of Pastoral Care
   Quotable Quotes on the Efficacy of Prayer 90
   Prayer: A Healer of the Ages 95
   Some General Principles for Praying with the Sick 97

  Prayers for Use in Hospital Ministry 98
    A Prayer for God's Providence 98
    A Prayer for God's Help 99
    A Prayer for Endurance 99
    A Prayer of Thanksgiving for Hospitals 100
    A Prayer for the Medical Professionals and Staff 100
    A Prayer Before Entering the Hospital 101
    A Prayer After Entering the Hospital 101
    A Prayer for Hope 101
    A Prayer for Strength 102
    A Prayer for God's Loving Presence 102
    A Prayer When Illness Is Minor 103
    A Prayer in a Time of Confusion 103
    A Prayer in a Time of Anxiety 103
    A Prayer When Human Help Fails 104
    A Prayer Before an Operation 104
    A Prayer After an Operation 104
    A Prayer for the Critically Ill 105
    A Prayer When Healing Is Delayed 105
    A Prayer for the Helpless and Bedridden 105
    A Prayer for the Puzzled and Perplexed 106
    A Prayer for One Injured by Accident 106
    A Prayer for One After Returning Home 106
    A Prayer for Family and Friends 107
    A Prayer for Other Patients 107
    A Prayer When Awaiting the Birth of a Child 108
    A Prayer After the Birth of a Child 108
    A Prayer at a Day's Beginning 108
    A Prayer at a Day's Conclusion 109
  Prayers of Various Faith Traditions 110
    Buddhist 110
    Christian (Catholic) 111
    Christian (Protestant) 112
    Hindu 113
    Islamic 114
    Jewish 115
    Native American 116
    Unitarian Universalist 117
Concluding Thoughts
  Relationships and Illness: A Paradox 121
Appendix
  Suggested Resources for Further Reading 128

Life in a Hospital: A Patient's Perspective

What Is a Hospital?

A HOSPITAL IS A PLACE of life and death. Most people in the United States are born in a hospital; most people in the United States die in a hospital. The beautiful and ugly seem to occur in hospitals.

Hospitalization is a time of celebration: Healthy babies are born; broken bones are mended; feared symptoms are diagnosed benign; pains are stilled. Hope abounds. God's goodness is apparent, or so it seems.

Hospitalization is a time of remorse: Babies are born dead or deformed; feared symptoms are confirmed. Hope is dashed. God is distant, or so it seems.

Hospitalization is a moment of preciseness: "As we suspected, you have a hot gall bladder. I can schedule you for surgery tomorrow, and you should be out of here by the end of the week."

Hospitalization is a time of disappointing impreciseness: "We're just not sure what's causing all this."

(Adapted from *Hospital Ministry* by Lawrence E. Holst)

A HOSPITAL IS A PLACE where people experience pain and suffering. However, these two terms are not synonymous. In fact, even though related, they are quite different. According to Rabbi Israel Kestenbaum, Founding Director of Jewish Institute for Pastoral Care in New York City:

> **Pain** is physiological, measurable, quantifiable;
>
> **Suffering** is a person's interpretation of and meaning of pain which is not reduced by medicines, but by transcendental realities – faith, hope, God...

This distinction is poignantly reflected in the many questions proposed and statements made by hospital patients:

"Something is happening to me that causes me pain."

"If there is someone who is in charge of all this, why is that someone allowing this to happen to me?"

"Suffering pain helps me identify with Jesus Christ."

"I don't even know if there is a god anymore."

"I know this is God's will."

A HOSPITAL IS A PLACE where the faith community needs strong representation, mainly from the clergy as the representatives of none other than God. The role, then, of the ministerial professional in such a setting is eloquently articulated by Eugene Peterson in his book, *Five Smooth Stones for Pastoral Work*:

"The task of pastoral care is to join the suffering, to enter the pain, to engage the absurdity, to descend into hell... not to minimize or to mitigate the suffering, but to help the sufferer to put the suffering into perspective."

Furthermore, in the words of Kahlil Gibran in *The Prophet*: **"Pain is the breaking of the shell that enslaves your understanding."** Ministerial presence at the bedside can facilitate this happening.

Finally, the National Institute for Healthcare Research featured an article reporting results of a recent survey conducted by Drs. Timothy Daaleman and Bruce Frey concerning the role of clergy in helping to meet patient needs. According to the text of the report entitled "Prevalence and Patterns of Physician Referral to Clergy and Pastoral Care Providers," *Archives of Family Medicine* (1998; 7:548-553), the doctors said: *"In medical settings, the providers of religion and spiritual interventions have a larger and more expanded role than previously reported."* The researchers went on to say that the growing partnership between doctors and pastoral care counselors parallels a new awareness of patients' desires to have their spiritual concerns addressed when dealing with illness. Additionally, according to an article in *Readers Digest*, October, 1999, entitled "Faith is Power Medicine," the author states that *"rewards of religion are becoming the stuff of science."* Similarly, Dr. Dale Matthews, Associate Professor of Medicine at Georgetown University Medical Center in Washington, D.C. and author of *The Faith Factor* said: *"We cannot prove scientifically that God heals, but I believe we can prove that belief in God has a beneficial effect. There's little doubt that healthy religious faith and practices can help people get better."*

> *"When one looks at it, one cannot see it.*
> *When one listens for it, one cannot hear it.*
> *However, when one uses it, it is inexhaustible."*
>
> Zen poem submitted by
> Lama Chuck Stanford, founder,
> Mindfulness Meditation Foundation

* Contributions by the author.

What Is a Hospital Patient?

The "Biotechnical model" (i.e. the patient is perceived as a machine that needs "fixing") views the patient as a single dimensional entity. Healing is perceived as correcting a biological dysfunction. A patient is, however, far more complex. Patients are people comprised of body, mind, spirit, and stories/memories (some of these, patients may have experienced in the hospital, a place where God was present with them) who have some form of illness which affects all aspects of the multidimensional whole. It is important to note that these various aspects of a patient are interdependent, interrelated links that are weakened with the onset of a serious illness. The degree, though, to which each link is weakened is unique to the patient in his or her own lived experiences. Therefore, this illness can be understood as brokenness with loss of integration in various aspects of wholeness:

- **Physical:** symptoms, signs, dysfunction

- **Mental:** deficient understanding of cause and effect

- **Emotional:** suffering, fear, anger, hurt, loss, grief, etc.

- **Social:** relationships – expectations, practices, roles

- **Spiritual:** meaning and purpose of life, future, hope, guilt, God

> *"The Tibetan (Buddhist) physician focuses his attention on spiritual factors even in the treatment of the simplest illnesses... The tradition is a holistic approach to the problem of suffering..."*
>
> Bonnie Pasqualoni

A strategy for healing must begin with an in-depth diagnosis. Who was the patient before the illness – physically, mentally, emotionally, socially, spiritually? Who is the patient now in these same areas? How does the patient see self? What are the perceived changes? How does the patient respond to these changes? What does the patient anticipate with "healing?" Who will the patient then be? Is that future self-picture realistic?

For holistic healing to occur, the multi-faceted aspects of a person's "brokenness" and subsequent "healing" should be addressed:

- **Physical** – This is primarily the responsibility of the patient's medical care team. However, there are non-medical areas of treatment that can be administered:

  - "Can I mow the yard for you?"

  - "Allow me to do the laundry and house cleaning."

- **Mental** – Non-understanding

  - "What would you like to know about your illness?"

  - "What about your illness troubles you?"

  - "Do you understand what your doctors are wanting to do, or <u>for you to do</u>?"

    - lose weight
    - stop smoking
    - exercise
    - radically alter lifestyle

- **Emotional** – Varied anxieties

  - "Would you like to share your concerns with me?"

  - "Hospitalization often causes sadness in people. Do you feel any sense of sadness?"

  - "Illness often causes fear. Has this been true for you?"

    - Fear of loss
    - Fear that people will not visit anymore

- Fear that I have lost control of life
- Fear that I might become an invalid
- Fear that I will die

❖ **Social** – support systems

- "Illness causes many people to feel alone. How is it with you?"
- "Has your family been able to visit during your illness?"
- "Who in your family has not visited you?" (It would be interesting to know what that says to the patient or how it is interpreted.)
- "Have your friends been able to visit during your illness?"
- "How does your family deal with illness?" (e.g. Do they talk about it? Do they sympathize with the sick?)

❖ **Spiritual** – matters of a divine nature

- "Where has God been during your illness?"
- "Has your illness altered your view of God?"
- "How do you cope with what has happened to you?"
- "As you look to the future, what do you see? Does that concern you?"

> *"Patients do not care how much you know until they know how much you care."*

The grids which follow reflect these multi-dimensional aspects of a patient with respect to wholeness and non-wholeness: 1) Unity of a patient; and 2) Characteristics of health/illness.

Unity of Patient

Brokenness	Healing
Physical	Anatomic and physiologic restoration Rehabilitation Change behavior as necessary
Mental	Correct data Identify thoughts Educate and teach
Emotional	Identify feelings Accept feelings without fear of judgment
Social	Own and be responsible for self Accept others Willingness to be open with boundaries
Spiritual	Hope restored Purpose and meaning of life clarified God is present and cares Forgiveness experienced

Characteristics of Health/Illness

Characteristic	Health	Illness
Self-Acceptance	Self-value	Self-shame
Community	Intimacy	Loneliness
Response to past	Forgiveness	Guilt
Future	Hope	Fear
View of death	Acceptance	Denial
Daily life	Enjoyment	Toleration

True healing means taking care of the whole person as is reflected in the grid (previous page) "Unity of Patient." This type of healing can succinctly be called "Whole Person Care." Especially in hospital and nursing home visitation, this ministry process allows for honest communication and the opportunity for patients to identify and own their feelings. It prompts discovery of unspoken needs and allows the patient to become an integral part of the plan of care. Whole person care facilitates an increased patient awareness of specific needs and helps the patient find areas of strength to compensate for the weaknesses. It helps to identify coping skills and techniques for handling stress.

Whole person care is resident within the pastoral caregiver who is friendly to, shows concern for, and is respectful of the patient. Furthermore, he or she must listen for clues that identify what may be the "real" patient concerns beyond the illness, if any. What is really going on? What do I sense is happening? Is there stress, fear, anxiety, depression, anger, distraction, fatigue, confusion, denial, or a combination of some of these emotions? How are things at home, on the job, with finances, in relationships with spouse/children/God/self?

Moreover, the helper must have the willingness and desire to be there for the patient, to explore these complex problems, even to be confrontive when necessary. A word of caution is in order about confrontation.

The patient must understand that he or she is accepted, respected, valued and loved, in order for confrontation to be viable in the healing process. Then, and only then, can things be said like, "Is that all that matters in your life?" or "I'm concerned that unless you deal with ... you will make little or no progress in your recovery." The effective pastoral caregiver, of necessity, exudes compassion for the one who is suffering, while at the same time, being a courageous person, willing to go where even "angels fear to tread."

The astute helper recognizes that people are more open to examining life's priorities, values systems and spirituality in times of crisis, and the helper is willing to facilitate that exploration. The result of such a process will be wholeness and integration of the patient, re-establishment of relationships, renewal of faith that leads to positive behavior.

The vast majority of this section has addressed issues of whole person care with respect to only patients. However, whole person care should include care for their families as well. When patients experience crisis, so do their families. And so, the onset of serious illness is a threat to the unity of the family system. The goal, then, of an all-encompassing model of whole person care is to help restore the unity of the family system, thereby strengthening the interrelated mind-body-spirit links.

One of these links, spirituality, is "the unifying force or vital principle of a person that integrates all other dimensions of the human being." Furthermore, "understanding spirituality has to do with understanding the whole of life." Therefore, the pastoral caregiver should be considered as an essential part of any healthcare team. The support that he or she can provide to both patient and family is needed for the maintenance of spiritual stability. "Spiritual stability exists when a balance exists among the life lived in the body, the life lived in the mind, and the life lived in the spirit." This "spirit of the whole of one's life" is kept alive by the pastoral caregiver's presence to support, listen and understand the stories of patients and patients' families. He or she can help them draw on individual or collective coping mechanisms to sustain spiritual stability.

Finally, based upon this discussion in its entirety, there seems to be little doubt that holistic healthcare extends well beyond the patient alone. Whole person care is for the patients and their families, helping to provide for:

- Acceptance of the past

- Direction for the present

- Courage for the future

* This section was adapted from materials from *The Medical Strategic Network*, an article entitled "Spirituality and the Use of an Intensive Care Unit On-Staff/On-Site Chaplain," by Patricia A. Angelucci, RN, MS, CCRN in *Critical Care Nurse*, Vol. 19, No. 4, August, 1999, and contributions by the author.

What Is It Like To Be Hospitalized?

This subject was discussed briefly in the previous section. However, its significance and importance for pastoral ministry demands amplification. This is especially true if Dr. Richard Dayringer (recently retired member of the Department of Medical Humanities, School of Medical Humanities, School of Medicine of Southern Illinois University and former Director of Pastoral Care and Chaplaincy at Baptist Hospital in Kansas City) assesses pastoral care correctly:

> *"An <u>art</u> more than a science, a <u>living relationship</u> more than a theoretical discipline, a <u>perspective</u> more than a category of work, a <u>way of being</u> more than a way of doing."*

Hospitalization is often a pivotal point in one's life, a kind of "rite of passage." What emerges from that experience will vary from person to person. For one, it will mean personal growth and transformation. For another, it will be an embittering, perplexing, or baffling period marked by prolific personal questioning: "Why has God put me here?" or "What does God want from me?" "What happens after I leave here?" These are only a few of the many questions patients will ask, the vast majority of which focus upon "the meaning of one's life." Some factors for the astute visitor to consider in determining this meaning of life are:

❖ The love of a family and one's love for the family

❖ A personally significant vocation

❖ Any successes achieved

❖ Acceptance of and by the community

❖ A sense of purpose: Being loved and used by God

(Concerning one's vocation, it would be important to know several things that directly relate to the hospitalization and convalescence. Is the patient fearful of losing a job? Is the patient going to be further behind at work and under pressure to "catch up?" Will the time off affect future promotions? Is the patient concerned that someone might be using his/her time away from the office for personal gain? How does the hospitalization/convalescence affect the workaholic Type A personality who is always "chomping at the bit?")

I think it is safe to say that the meaning of one's life is questioned, at least emotionally, by everyone during crises. A "life review" seems to be a natural part of illness and hospitalization.

Hospitalization as a "rite of passage" (a phrase introduced earlier in this discussion) has several phases:

- ❖ **Separation** – from home, family, friends, pets, and belongings that are familiar. This "isolation," as another writer suggests, is perhaps the chief characteristic of one's being hospitalized.

- ❖ **Betwixt and Between** – a "land" of little familiarity: medical tests, treatments, surgery, etc. (i.e. a place where patients surrender control of their lives)

- ❖ **Clarity** – in the "real" reason for the hospitalization

- ❖ **New Vision** – of what lies ahead

The phases of "clarity" and "new vision" may well, and often do, heighten the crisis of illness. For example, major spiritual and emotional crises of illness normally occur:

- Before surgery

- During a period of long convalescence

- When facing life with a handicap

- When being told of a terminal diagnosis

- Near death / when dying

However, human companionship and pleasant visits to which the patient can look forward and enjoy are the best treatments known for these spiritual crises.

A clergy person's presence with the sick and hospitalized is an indication of the love and caring interest of the faith community for the patient. It implies and points to the love of God for the sick and family. Finally, these pastoral visits can be helpful in enabling the patient to attach some form of "meaning" to the physical condition and situation.

> *"Basically there are two perpetual streams of love in this world. The one is man's love for God; the other is God's love for man."*
>
> Swami Satprakashananda

* This section was adapted from materials contained in *How to Make Pastoral Calls* by Russell L. Dicks; *Lay Shepherding* by Rudolph E. Grantham; and "Hospital Ministry Guidelines" by J. Thomas Meigs and contributions by the author.

The Attachment of Meaning and Purpose to Illness

There is perhaps no more relevant factor in a patient's illness experience than the meaning that he or she attaches to it. There are at least ten frames of reference from which a human being can view illness:

- Illness as challenge
- Illness as enemy
- Illness as punishment
- Illness as weakness
- Illness as relief or rest
- Illness as strategy
- Illness as irreparable loss or damage
- Illness as value
- Illness as a natural consequence
- Illness as blessing

Usually the meaning of illness or wellness relates directly to a person's perception of the purpose of his or her life. Every patient has some idea of what life is for, although few may be in the habit of articulating such thoughts. This element relates in part to learned values (cultural, ethnic, racial, gender, socio-economic) but is rooted in a deeper, more personal sense of priorities.

Such thoughts and perceptions will substantially influence the meaning and purpose the patient attaches to his or her illness. For example, if one is aware of a personal behavior or attitude that violates one's sense of purpose in life, an illness may be perceived as a form of punishment.

Similarly, some patients may regard a return to health as a means to reaching more ultimate goals in their lives, whereas others may perceive health as an end in itself. The need to attach a meaning to all events appears to be a universal human experience.

---

* This section was adapted from materials submitted by Clifford C. Kuhn, M.D., Professor of Psychiatry, University of Louisville Medical School and contributions by the author.

Patient's Needs – Another Viewpoint

The predominant emotions experienced by patients upon entering the hospital are **fear** with its cousin, **anxiety**. They are present to a greater or lesser degree in all patients. Fear and anxiety commonly take primarily four forms, according to Richmond and Middleton and their use of various surveys.

- **The Fear and Anxiety of Separation** -- Admission to the hospital requires that we leave the company of those who love us and abide for a while in a land of strangers. These strangers come to us dressed in a manner different from any garb to which we are accustomed outside the hospital (e.g. masked or gloved which can tend to intensify the feeling of separation). They speak a language that we often do not understand. They communicate with one another in hushed tones, frequently in our presence, making us wonder what they are discussing. When they do not want us to hear them, they leave the room to talk about us. Is it any wonder that patients often say, "I just want to go home!" Even when the reason for hospitalization is a happy one, such as the delivery of a baby, there is still a deep desire to "be at home in my own bed."

- **The Fear and Anxiety of Dependence** -- The hospital is a place that teaches people – some for the first time since infancy – the meaning of dependence. We depend upon the admitting department to have a room for us, on the dietary department to feed us, on the diagnostic and therapeutic skills of the medical and nursing staff to treat us, on the training of social workers and therapists to ensure our continued healing upon discharge, on chaplains to understand our feelings and to provide pastoral support for our emotional and spiritual needs. Surgery requires us to depend on an anesthesiologist to put us to sleep and wake us up, and on a surgeon to cut us open and successfully put us back together again.

- **The Fear and Anxiety of Losing Control** -- Upon entering the hospital, patients quickly surrender control. Loss of control begins with the "see-through" gown that is given to patients to wear. Patients eat when the hospital determines and may share a room with a stranger (who may snore loudly or watch television all night.) Everyone from the newspaper sales person to the attending physician enters the room without so much as a knock. Body secretions are examined and measured. Control of the most vital functions, including stopping and starting the heart, is surrendered to others. Children are particularly vulnerable to the fear of losing control. To the degree that they can be included in the decisions that are made about them, they tend to do better emotionally.

- ❖ **The Fear and Anxiety of Pain and Death** — Many persons worry about their ability to tolerate pain. Males who have been schooled to ignore pain may fear being judged weak or whiny. Beyond the pain is the ever-present fear of death. Patients often remark that "hospitals are places where people go to die." Even ostensibly happy occasions, such as childbirth, are marked by the concern that "the baby will have all of his fingers and toes" (i.e. desire for the "perfect" baby).

All these fears and anxieties add up to taking people out of homes in which they feel secure and placing them into a stressful and strange environment in which they feel threatened, the victim of forces beyond their control. (A side note from this is that there are some people from dysfunctional families/marriages who see hospitalization as a reprieve or a "time-out.") Given the known deleterious effects that such stress can have upon such persons, there are some who feel that the fact that people regain their health in the hospital is less a testimony to the skill of the medical profession and more the evidence of the remarkable resilience of the human body and spirit.

* Material adapted from *The Pastor and the Patient: A Practical Guidebook for Hospital Visitation* by Kent D. Richmond and David L. Middleton along with contributions by the author.

Insights of and Strategies for Pastoral Care in a Hospital Setting

Pastoral Care: A Noble Ministry With a Rich Tradition

Hospitalized persons need much more than physical care for wholeness in healing to occur. That's where the pastoral care comes in. Pastoral care has existed for millennia as a significant part of the varied religious traditions of the world. However, this ministry was not (and is not) always administered by ordained clergy. The "cure and care of souls" has been exercised on myriads of occasions by ordinary people to relieve a multitude of maladies affecting persons of every nationality, race, gender, and religious persuasion. Pastoral care, then, whether performed by the professional clergy or layperson, is to fulfill a high calling dating back over thousands of years. How is that calling defined? There are many ways to define pastoral care; I have chosen to share one offered by Clebsch and Jaeckle in *Pastoral Care in Historical Perspective*.

> *"Pastoral care consists of helping acts, done by representative persons directed toward the healing, sustaining, guiding, reconciling of troubled persons whose troubles arise in the context of ultimate meanings and concerns."*

Accordingly, pastoral care is administered by a person or persons representing a faith tradition or community. This ministry calls forth questions and issues of deepest meaning and highest concern of a patient, for it is practiced at a depth where the meaning of life itself and faith is involved on the part of not only the patient, but the caregiver as well. Therefore, genuine pastoral care is far more than a "friendly visit" to someone in the hospital. On the contrary, it is, in the best way possible, to enter the world of the patient to facilitate healing, sustaining, guiding, and/or reconciling. Dietrich Bonhoeffer, a Christian theologian, speaks of Christ "pro me" (for me). In the same way, pastoral care is _for_ the patient.

- **Healing** is the ministerial task that seeks to help an ill or diseased person achieve wholeness. This wholeness, though, does not necessarily mean physical wholeness, although that is most certainly a part of healing. Pastoral healing may well include counsel to and encouragement for the patient to take medications, undergo surgery, begin to exercise and change an unhealthy lifestyle as a means of restoring physical health. In such a pastoral role, it may be possible to think of this in terms of "casting out" disease through surgery, IVs, pharmaceuticals, nutriceuticals, etc. On the other hand, the more primary function of pastoral healing is to help the troubled person achieve a new level of spiritual insight and well-being (i.e. to enable the patient to look upon the experience as a meaningfully significant spiritual chapter in his or her life). It is noteworthy to mention that healing operates in circumstances when a loss is recovered or the damage is reparable. Healing may even happen, though, when death occurs.

- **Sustaining** is a ministry of helping a person deal with an overwhelming sense of loss, such as the death of a loved one. Typically, sustaining includes four processes:

  1. **Preservation** – This aspect of sustaining seeks to minimize any further loss or excessive retreat. Its goal is to help the sufferer "hold the line." The methods of preservation are varied and many – a simple touch, caring/reassuring words, physical presence.

  2. **Consolation** – Relief from the misery of irretrievable loss, or what is initially perceived as irretrievable loss, is the function of consolation. (Interestingly, adequate pastoral care can sometimes help a person see the same data with a new perspective.) In this pastoral mode, the minister helps to assure the one who is in pain that he or she is still in the company of the living. The pastoral figure does not, though, minimize or negate the damaging loss. On the contrary, the one suffering the tragic loss is assured by the minister of God's concern and presence even in the midst of the loss. Whereas preservation seeks to arrest regression, consolation provides a sense of comfort that began and increased during the regression.

  3. **Consolidation** – This act of sustaining attempts to put the suffering into the perspective of living. Resources are gathered;

mobilization takes place. For example, a bereaved widow comes to the point of seeing that she has children to live for. The pastoral role is to help the troubled person establish some foundation for reconstruction of life.

4. **Redemption** – The loss is embraced, and the building of an ongoing life in pursuit of fulfillment is engaged. The pastor hopes to help the person achieve spiritual growth as well as a positive outlook on life.

❖ **Guiding** is the function of pastoral care in assisting patients or other perplexed people to make confident choices between alternative courses of thought, action, and/or treatment. Guiding proceeds down a number of roads from advice-giving to listening and reflecting. The former (advice-giving) resides primarily in the helper and is useful and necessary at times. The latter (listening and reflecting) involves the helper in facilitating the one being helped to come up with the resolution to the difficulty. How important is listening?

Note these words of Dietrich Bonhoeffer:

> *"He who can no longer listen to his brother will soon be no longer listening to God."*

Whatever the pastoral method employed in guiding, the ultimate goal is to gently lead people to some sense of self-understanding that will result in a decision.

❖ **Reconciling** – Reconciling seeks to re-establish broken relationships between fellow human beings and between people and God. Two of the modes employed to bring about reconciliation of alienated people are **forgiveness** and **implementation of change**.

Forgiveness between people can be brought about through vocal expressions or some type of nonverbal communication; in the case of one's relationship to God, the same might take place in the context of worship through a sacrament/ordinance or prayer. A pastoral figure plays a key role in this aspect of reconciling, especially at the bedside of patients who may well believe that their "sins" have caused God to punish them.

Implementation of change as a mode of reconciling means leading people into situations and thought processes where relationships can be re-established. On the part of the pastoral caregiver, this may evoke a word of correction, counsel toward confession, repentance, change in lifestyle, or exhortation to remain in the faith community as a way to resist temptation. One of the major afflictions of human beings is guilt. Thus, the need for a ministry of reconciliation is an absolute essential.

Finally, as a minister who seeks to bring about healing, sustaining, guiding, and reconciliation for hurting people, it is of paramount importance that the pastoral care person be sensitive to and follow God's leadership in this noble calling. <u>Compassion</u>, <u>integrity</u>, and an "<u>other-centeredness</u>" are vital character attributes of one who administers pastoral care.

* This section was adapted from materials contained in "Part 3: The Four Pastoral Functions," *Pastoral Care in Historical Perspective* by William A. Clebsch and Charles R. Jaeckle and contributions by the author.

The Hospital Needs You!

The Doctor Needs You!

The Nurse Needs You!

The Patient Needs You!

The ABC's of Hospital Visitation

The hospital room is to be considered as private as the home. Therefore, unless you are visiting your spouse, dependent child, or aged parent, it would be more appropriate if you would consider yourself as a guest, albeit a welcome one. [It is noteworthy that there might be times when the pastor is not welcome or a visit might be strenuous for him or her. For example, a sense of unwelcomeness may be experienced when there is a strained relationship between church/pastor and patient. A visit might be tension-filled for the pastor when someone in the patient's family has an "agenda" and wants the pastor to address it with the patient (e.g. smoking, drinking, spiritual condition, pray with a certain conclusion).] In order to make your visit as helpful and meaningful as possible for the patient, the four following suggestions are offered:

Focus Upon the Environment

❖ **Time Factors**

- **Time of day** – Normal visiting hours are best, although many hospitals today do not have regularly stated visiting hours. Even so, there are still better times to visit than others. Mornings are usually filled with testing and doctor visits. Therefore, afternoons are usually a more suitable time for a quality visit. Try not to visit at mealtimes. However, if you do show up and the patient is eating, insist that the patient continue with the meal. Also, the ideal time for pre-surgical visits is two hours prior on the day of surgery. However, a pastoral visit is still quite effective at some time during the day before the surgery.

- **Length of visit** – How long you stay in the room is usually determined by your closeness to the patient, the patient's physical/emotional condition, and the purpose of the visit. To some patients, we are a necessary source of strength; to others, a good friend who "wears like an old shoe;" and still to others, a guest who must be entertained. Generally speaking, limit your visit to a brief period of time. Visits tire patients even though they may be greatly appreciated. However, do not "rush" the visit because it might be perceived as simply one of duty rather than of concern or caring. Do leave, though, when you say you are leaving.

- ❖ **At the door** – Pay careful attention to any signs that may be posted and respectfully comply with that information. If a "No Visitors" sign is posted, leave a note with the nurse that says something very special about how you are feeling toward the patient. Upon entering, knock firmly but gently and <u>identify yourself</u>.

- ❖ **In the room** – Be aware of the condition of the patients if you are visiting in a semi-private room. No "gang visiting." It is possible for more than two or three people to overwhelm the emotional capacity of the patient.

Focus Upon the Patient

- ❖ Take a position in line with the patient's vision, but stay away from windows, if possible. A glare can ensue and prevent the patient from clearly seeing you.

- ❖ Do not lean on or sit on the bed unless the patient asks for you to do so. Even then, your restraint from doing so is best.

- ❖ Let the patient offer to shake hands with you. Be sensitive of the "tenderness to the touch" that the patient might experience. Having said that, though, touch is important to many patients. It communicates that you truly care for them. Unfortunately, people with certain diseases that are <u>not</u> infectious report that "no one will touch me."

- ❖ Use prayer when requested or according to your religious tradition. Prayers should be specific, positive, and short. Prayers should include intercession for patient, express concern for family, and ask for skill, wisdom, and discernment for the medical staff.

- ❖ Keep reports of bad news to a bare minimum.

- ❖ Do not engage in discussions about controversial issues or "hot" topics.

- Do not whisper in the room to other visitors or medical staff; the patient will think you are talking about him or her.

- Offer medical information sparingly. Never destroy the patient's faith in the doctor or medical staff.

- Do not discuss medications unless you are a medical professional – doctor, nurse, pharmacist.

- Do not share "war stories" of others' experiences in similar circumstances.

- Do not ask the diagnosis; it could be embarrassing.

- Observe signs of patient discomfort.

Focus Upon Yourself

- **Be relaxed** – it is best not to visit if you are tired, depressed, or sick.

- **Be cheerful** – do not force cheerfulness, though, if you do not feel it.

- **Note your own feelings** – anxiety, boredom, anger. These feelings tell you how you are reacting to the situation or they may be the feelings of the patient resonating in you.

Focus Upon Your Purpose

Most patients are too sick to entertain visitors. The purpose of a pastoral visit is not to be entertained or to socialize. It is to be a visit of support as evidence of the concept that "visitation is a ministry of love." Therefore, the specific purpose of a pastoral visit should be directly related to the patient's need – physical, emotional and/or spiritual – as a communication of genuine concern from the faith community.

> * This section was adapted from materials contained in *Lay Shepherding* by Rudolph E. Grantham and contributions by the author.

Nuances of Nursing Home Ministry

A vast majority of the previous discussion ("The ABC's of Hospital Visitation") applies equally to visitation and ministry in a nursing home facility. However, there are additional factors to consider.

Many nursing home residents have no home; others will never be able to return to their homes. Therefore, depression and a sense of hopelessness are more commonplace in this type of facility. Furthermore, many of the residents experience a heightened degree of frustration as a result of the physical limitations imposed by weakened bodies. The emotional/social shock and spiritual resignation from such a perspective can be overwhelming. It is no wonder, then, that a significant number of these individuals view their residence as the "last stop before death."

For the reasons previously stated, the following variations from and additions to "The ABC's…" can be thought of as a means to provide a sense of hopefulness and community for the patients in a residential care facility.

- Visits can be longer.

- Visit at mealtimes. For many people, the meal was a family and social "happy hour." A visit at such a time could help rekindle the pleasant memories of those past experiences.

- Comment on pictures or personal objects in the room. "Who or what is this…" can jump-start conversations.

- Host a church service from start to finish; escort residents to and from the worship area.

- Be or provide a guest speaker for programs at the facility (e.g. "Chaplain Chat" program). The presenter could provide a special story, song, skit, or poem with an appropriate religious message.

- Provide for a music ministry program; share the talents of the musically inclined of your congregation. Many residents in nursing home facilities thoroughly enjoy music.

- ❖ Encourage youth and children to become involved in ministry to the elderly shut-ins. They will be greatly appreciated and make their audiences laugh and smile unlike anything that adults can accomplish.

- ❖ Provide person-to-person conversation (even when involved in a group program). It makes a big difference in the life of a resident when special attention is given specifically to him or her.

Desirable Qualities of People Performing Nursing Home Ministry

- ❖ Empathy for multiple losses: physical, social, etc.

- ❖ Compassion and genuine desire to serve the needs of others

- ❖ Sensitivity to faith diversities

- ❖ Flexibility with various situations that may occur

* This section was adapted from materials contained in *Lay Shepherding* by Rudolph E. Grantham along with suggestions submitted by Mark Fenton and the author.

Visiting the Sick or Shut-In: A Checklist of Things To Consider

Do not stay too long, particularly on a hospital visit. Make the period very short if the person is in critical condition or appears very tired. Frequently five or ten minutes are enough for someone who is acutely ill.

Be aware that patients will sometimes act in aberrant ways, not only because of shock or the effects of illness, but also because of medications.

Sit in a place where you can be seen easily. If the person is not able to roll over or sit up, remain standing so she or he can look at you without tiring. However, don't stand in the path of sunlight or other bright light. Also, suggest to a patient that you pull a curtain between the two of you and the next bed, to offer more privacy.

Suggest a change of scene. In a hospital or nursing home, suggest to an ambulatory patient that the two of you go to a waiting room, lounge, cafeteria, chaplain's room, or some other place. If it is not possible to leave a hospital room, be aware of the needs of any other patients in the room who could be very sick or in great pain.

It is best to visit a hospital patient during visiting hours, although many hospitals today do not have "regular" visiting hours. Even so, when you have arrived outside the room, check with the ward nurse or attendant to see if the patient is receiving visitors; some people do not want to see anyone when they are ill. Knock on the door before you enter. If medical personnel arrive to perform certain procedures, excuse yourself and return when they have finished. If the person falls asleep, leave a note and return at another time.

If you wish to offer help, be specific. For example, to a young mother in the hospital: "Would you like me to drive your daughter to school?"; or to a shut-in who has twisted her ankle: "I'd like to bring in supper tomorrow evening; is that okay?"

The care you give is not just for the person in the bed, but also for the relatives and close friends of the sick. Part of your time may be spent with them. Do remember, though, that the last "sense" people lose is their hearing. So, be careful when talking in a quiet voice to nurses or relatives. Hushed conversations can indicate to the sick individual – even one who is comatose – that things are worse than they seem, that death may be around the corner. When speaking to the patient, adjust your voice level to the individual's hearing, especially if he or she wears a hearing aid. It is helpful occasionally to ask if you are speaking too softly (or too loudly).

Make your inquiry of the patient to others in the room in a personal manner "How is John/Jean doing?" not "How is he/she doing?"

Use physical gestures to express your caring – touching, patting, stroking, squeezing, religious signs, and so forth. Be sensitive, though, not to cross boundaries in this area.

When praying, listen to the patient's requests. Do not assume you know what they are. Ask, "What concerns would you like to bring to the Lord?" Invite the person to join you in offering prayers.

Encourage hope without giving false assurances. One good rule is to enter the room with a cheerful, but serious mood tone expressing no excessive joy or sympathy. It is better for you to adjust to the patient's mood than for him or her to adjust to yours. Remember, that this could shift radically from visit to visit.

Listen carefully to what is concerning or upsetting the person, and do not make assumptions about what might be the problem.

Try to help the person relax, and use your time effectively. Many sick people may not know how to act during your visit, especially those who are not close to the church or if you are new on the church staff. So, be sensitive to this possibility. Also, be aware that your presence could even spell impending doom, a sign that things are worse than they really are.

Prepare yourself to work with the sick, especially in hospitals or nursing homes. If you find the institutional atmosphere difficult to handle, you would do well to "desensitize" yourself to it by touring a local hospital with a hospital chaplain or fellow clergy person.

Approach the visits in a relaxed manner, spending time, asking questions, and making repeated calls until the surroundings are more comfortable to you. You also need to realize that visiting the sick can drain you emotionally. If you are making a great many calls, be aware of "burn-out." (An example of a tell-tale sign of burn-out is that visitation has become a duty and not a caring ministry.) Finally, of utmost importance and a great source of strength, keep your personal relationship with God fresh.

Do not try to make people feel guilty for being sick or dying. Unfortunately, there are some who use a hospital visit to tell a patient that illness or accidents result from some sinful act.

When making institutional visits, it is frequently helpful to gain information from doctors, nurses, or attendants about the person's condition. This is an opportunity for you to find out their suggestions for helping the patient or resident; they can tell you, for example, if he or she has been depressed, very lonely, and so on. Do not ask a patient about the diagnosis or prognosis. It is better to ask, "How are things going?" or a similar open-ended question.

Openly acknowledging the urine bag, the artificial leg, and so on, helps relieve any embarrassment or emotional discomfort caused by such conditions with many patients.

Thoroughly wash your hands before and after the visit.

Do not bring the sick or shut-in your diseases. If you have the flu or anything contagious, stay home.

Calls on the sick or shut-in can be expected or unannounced. Each way has its advantages or disadvantages. Do remember that, for an especially lonely or bored patient, your visit is eagerly anticipated. It is also usually best, and always polite, to telephone a shut-in at home before your visit. Additionally, advance notice to nursing home staff may be beneficial, especially if the resident will need assistance with personal grooming.

Do not apologize for not coming sooner or more often. An apology requires some sort of response from the other person.

Sick people frequently like variety and change. A little surprise is always nice. Occasionally drop in at unusual times. Wear something bright or humorous like a Hawaiian shirt. Bring a library book, CD, cartoon (maybe a Xerox copy, perhaps enlarged; it could be a conversation starter for others who see it) or inexpensive gift.

Visiting the sick is no time to tell "horror stories" you have heard, such as Aunt Tillie who "had the same thing, God rest her soul."

Do a lot of listening. Sometimes the sick want nothing more than someone with whom they feel comfortable, who will sit by them, and be present without much talk.

Do not play doctor. Do not answer medical questions such as, "When will I get well?" or "How serious is it?" A patient who wants specific information on his or her condition can be urged to make a list of questions and ask the physician. You can then respond to the feelings of fear or uncertainty that underlie these questions.

Try not to show horror or shock on your face when you see a person who is disfigured, has a foul-smelling cancer, burns, serious injuries, or other extreme condition. Do not pretend it doesn't exist; just try to be undisturbed by it, and focus on the person's needs. If you have difficulty in such situations, "desensitize" yourself by gradually increasing exposures. Practice being relaxed in your visits by making your physical movements smooth and not sharp or jerky.

Make use of chaplains. They can make visits when you cannot, alert you to problems that exist, and obtain information about a patient that you might otherwise be unable to learn. They can also act as advocates for the patient with the medical staff.

---

* This section was adapted from materials contained in *The Caring Church* by Howard Stone along with contributions by the author.

Practical Suggestions for Hospital Visitation

Before the Visit

- Find out a convenient time to call.
- Check with the attending nurse.
- Visit when well; if you are ill, do not go.
- Remember that the patient's condition is personal.
- Consider the patient's rights.
- Keep personal problems to yourself.

During the Visit

- Enter the room only if the call light above the door is not on.
- Knock before entering the room.
- Pause for a moment to see what is going on in the room. What do you see? Hear? Smell? Sense?
- Walk and talk softly.
- Attempt to be neutral in mood, with a little emphasis on the cheerful.
- Have a pleasant facial expression.
- Identify yourself clearly: wear a name badge; provide a business card (perhaps one that is folded and will "stand up" on the bedside table for greater visibility).
- Maintain eye contact.

- ❖ Acknowledge the presence of others in the room.
- ❖ Be sensitive to the "gang" visitation syndrome; offer to leave.
- ❖ Stand or sit in a position where the patient can easily focus on you.
- ❖ Shake hands only at the patient's initiative.
- ❖ Give the patient a chance to talk.
- ❖ If the conversation lags or patient becomes restless, prepare to leave.
- ❖ Be brief in your visit.
- ❖ When ready to leave, leave; do not linger.

* Adapted from materials from Dr. Jim Hightower, Director of Pastoral Counseling at the McFarland Institute, New Orleans, Louisiana, *How to Make Pastoral Calls* by Russell L. Dicks and contributions by the author.

Nurses Speak Out

The following material is a series of responses to two questions asked of nurse managers and staff nurses from various patient-care units at Shawnee Mission Medical Center: 1) What are some things that visiting clergy should know and practice that would facilitate close working relationships between nurse and pastor? 2) What are some things for visiting clergy to consider in order to maximize their visits with patients?

❖ **Things that facilitate the development of close working relationships with nurses on the units where clergy visit patients:**

- Check with attending nurse to see what is happening with and perceived needs of patient so you will not be "blind-sided."

- Be aware that nurses have multiple responsibilities for several patients and may not be readily available to converse with you. Therefore, be patient with them.

- Refer any patient-care related issues to the attending nurse (e.g. something to eat/drink, use of restroom facilities, changing positions in bed).

- Do not touch medical treatment equipment; call for nurse's assistance.

- Be sensitive to the emotional and spiritual needs of the medical staff. When patients are critically ill and die, staff grieves, also.

- Notify attending nurse of any religious ritual (e.g. anointing, last rites, communion, baptism, etc.) performed with a patient so that such can be documented in patient's chart for the purpose of enabling any member of the attending medical team to share the ritual with family members not present at the time, if they should inquire.

- As much as possible, respect regular visiting hours, especially during shift change times.

> *"Cultivate relationships with nurses who have a wealth of knowledge to share with you."*
>
> Robin Williams as Patch Adams
> from the movie by the same name

❖ Items to consider for maximizing clergy visits with parishioners:

- Be sensitive to needs and concerns of family members and close friends as well as those of the patient; these needs can be spiritual, emotional or even physical (e.g. food in the home, transportation to and from the hospital for visitation, care of small children or someone else for whom the family member is responsible).

- Pray with patient, family, and attending nurse, if present.

- Be conscious of and respectful of signs on the door of the patient's room (e.g. "NPO" – no food or drink; "Visitation limited to family;" "Check at the nurses' station before entering room;" and "Isolation").

- Remember that your presence is not only representative of God but the community of faith as well. "My church visited me today," when it was simply a visit by the pastor.

- Allow the patient to "tell his or her story" and encourage this by various rhetorical devices and body language.

- Leave a business card or some identifying item indicating a "church visit" as a way of relating to family members not present that you <u>had</u> been there, even if the patient does not remember and responded with "No" when asked.

- Sit down (i.e. "Be there" with the patient in the room), but ask first if it will be all right for you to sit and visit.

- Afternoons are, generally speaking, the best times for a visit because the mornings are often filled with doctors' visits and tests being performed. Furthermore, the patient may be more rested in the afternoon which can facilitate a better visit.

- Acknowledge other patients in the room, if any.

- Knock before entering a room, and identify yourself.

- Especially in the Emergency Department, ICU, or any other area where a patient may be in immediate crisis, encourage and help direct family members or friends to an area outside the patient-care area, thereby allowing the medical staff to serve the patient more adequately. However, it is important in these times for you, or in coordination with a staff chaplain, if present, to communicate information from the medical team to the patient's loved ones.

- If certain family members feel a strong need to be in the patient-care area when emergency treatment is being performed (and that need is well understood), encourage them to request permission from the attending physician or nurse.

- Stay with the family for support in crisis or bereavement situations.

* Contributions by the author.

Perspectives on Ministry of Presence

"Pastoral care emphasizes 'being' rather than 'doing.' Pastoral presence is a truly powerful and holy manifestation of pastoral care... and meaningful to others... and should be practiced actively."

> Dr. Larry J. Austin, ACPE Supervisor and Director of Spiritual Care, Shore System of Maryland, "Just Being There: The Power of Pastoral Presence." *Chaplaincy Today* 14:1, 1998

"Don't just stand there, do something," says society. "Don't do something, just stand there is the role of pastoral care."

> Rev. Jerry Kolb, Retired CPE Supervisor and Director of the Pastoral Care Department, Saint Luke's Hospital of Kansas City, Missouri

"The Church and those affiliated with it symbolize God and God's special efforts to bring health, relief and comfort to suffering people. It is not the words spoken but the presence felt that makes God real in times of illness."

> Russell L. Dicks, *How to Make Pastoral Calls*

"Presence has been described as being there and being with someone for the purpose of meeting healthcare needs. When presence occurs, dispiriting factors such as vulnerability and isolation are lessened."

> Patricia A. Angelucci, RN, MS, CCRN, Nurse Manager in the medical / surgical / neurological intensive care unit at Abbott-Northwestern Hospital, Minneapolis, Minnesota, *Critical Care Nurse*, Vol. 19, No. 4, August, 1999; 63

"Presence means listening in a way that involves giving of one's self and being there in a way that the other person describes as meaningful."

> J. Pettigrew quoted in an article by Patricia A. Angelucci, *Critical Care Nurse*, Vol. 19, No. 4, August, 1999; 64

"Presence is the physical being there and the psychological being with a patient."

> J. L. Shaffer quoted in an article by Patricia A. Angelucci, *Critical Care Nurse*, Vol. 19, No. 4, August, 1999; 64

Importance of the Ministry of Presence

Illness and disease are not confined exclusively to the body. On the contrary, sickness spreads to a person's emotional and spiritual life. Thus, the physical pain is transformed into emotional and spiritual suffering and vice versa.

Dr. Larry Dossey, author of *Meaning and Medicine,* views our bodies as more like music than an object. According to Dossey, the body "is a harmony of movements and patterns that flows in and out of the harmonies emitted by those around us, including plants and animals." "This condition of harmony," he goes on to say, "is often called 'wellness' or, simply, 'health,' which is a constant and continuous dynamic process, like an unfinished symphony."

Based upon Dossey's observations, it seems fair to assume that a "ministry of presence" of competent, professional caregivers is an absolute essential for wholeness in healing to take place.

This "Presence" Means Being:

- Aware of the dignity of a patient's life, the entire self
- In attendance to the patient
- In the here and now with the patient
- Prompt to act on an expressed or implied need of the patient
- Sensitive to the moment and it's implications to what is happening

* Contributions by the author.

Additional Thoughts on the Ministry of Presence: Being There While You Are There

> *"We walk alongside them, not trying to fix their situation or pain, but rather trying instead to comfort."*

- ❖ **Be Prepared.** Take a few moments to collect your thoughts. It might be in your car, in the hospital chapel, or a place where you are able to shut out the rest of the world and diminish your anxieties. Pray that your presence will convey to the patients that you are here; you want to be here with them; you are concerned; and God is concerned.

- ❖ **Be Present.** Our attitude is primary. If we really do not want to be there in the room in the first place, then we may act unknowingly, relay disinterest, display unavailability, and pace with hurriedness. We may come across as doing a chore, rather than ministering attentively. Center attention upon the people you have come to see and follow their responses with close attention, close thoughtfulness, and close concern. The patients are your most important focus for these moments. Watch for "mind wandering." We can waste a good bit of time and an opportunity to show God's love and concern when we do not pay attention effectively. Another way to communicate "presence" with the patient is whether we stand or sit during the visit. Dr. Harold Ivan Smith, a prolific writer and popular speaker on grief, stated the following about the need for some patients to have the visitor sit down: "My dad and mom, through his many hospitalizations, commented on the people who didn't sit down or 'didn't stay long enough to take their coat off.'"

> *"To comfort often, to care always defines the 'Ministry of Presence.'"*

- **Be Open.** Listen to what the patients have to say <u>without evaluation</u>. Meet them where they are and in whatever mood they present themselves. Do not look for answers. This puts you in a "fix it" mode when they simply want to be heard, not "fixed." Many times, more healing goes on when we are listening than when we are talking.

- **Be Sensitive** to their needs and condition. Ask yourself if there is an underlying meaning or theme to their words. Care is to have a "feel for." For example, if the patient says, "I just don't want to be a burden to anyone," what does that really mean? Care is to have a "feel for them." Always remember that caring and sensitivity supersede any techniques.

- **Be Supportive** while being human. Do not "back off" because you are afraid of not knowing what to say. It is okay to admit you do not have all the answers. "I don't understand why this is happening to you either" is far better than any attempt to offer an explanation for the patient's condition. By all means, avoid statements like "I know just how you feel," because you do not; no one knows but the patient and God.

> *"The most terrible disease of all is indifference."*
>
> Robin Williams as Patch Adams
> from the movie by the same name

---

* This section was adapted from materials contained in the "Be" attitudes section of *Bedside Manners: A Practical Guide to Visiting the Sick* by Katie Maxwell, *How to Make Pastoral Calls* by Russell L. Dicks, along with suggestions provided by J. Thomas Meigs and the author.

Humor: A Good Medicine for Suffering

When you genuinely care for someone, you want to do something, to, for, or with that person to make what is, or perceived as, a bad situation better. In settings like hospitals, nursing homes, or even funeral homes where people are suffering, one of the best things you can provide is humor, for it is "good medicine."

> *"Humor can brighten another person's day. The right topics help people to open up, to share their dreams, their fantasies and brighten up for one brief moment where they don't concentrate on pain; they don't even feel the pain."*
>
> Robin Williams as Patch Adams
> from the movie by the same name

> *"Laughter relaxes arteries, speeds up the heart, decreases blood pressure, which has positive effects on cardiovascular and respiratory ailments, as well as increasing the immune system response."*
>
> Robin Williams as Patch Adams
> from the movie by the same name;
> confirmed by Ray E. Lash, M.D., Cardiology Services, P.A., Shawnee Mission, Kansas

For many years as a pastor, and now as a hospital chaplain, I have used humor in ministry with hospital patients, nursing home residents, and families grieving the death of loved ones. "Humor me," if you will, and allow me to share a few experiences on the use of humor.

One day I received a referral that a patient wanted to complete an Advance Directive (not only did he complete one for himself, but his wife completed one for herself – a double!) I learned in that initial visit that Mr. S. was scheduled for bypass surgery the following day. As you can imagine, he was apprehensive and fearful. In my several visits with him prior to his surgery, I found that humor lessened his anxiety considerably; he enjoyed our exchanges of jokes and stories. On the morning of his surgery, I stopped in for one last visit for prayer and an offer of encouragement for the outcome of the surgery. Before leaving, though, I said: "No jokes for the next couple of days!" He laughed, but also knew the reason for that statement. Coughing, laughing, or anything that causes excessive movement in the chest area following open-heart surgery is not very pleasant. In fact, it is quite painful. The use of humor must be appropriately timed.

On another similar occasion with an open-heart surgery patient, the use of humor was not only good for the patient but the patient's family as well. Mrs. R. had successful surgery but was not recovering as expected due to other physical problems. As a result of all of this, she became depressed and was beginning to give up hope. What could I do to help her and her family? You guessed it – humor. I made her laugh. In fact, I was the only one who could make her smile. However, I also had a number of serious times with her talking about issues of ultimate concern with critically ill people. Mrs. R., her children, and I laughed and grieved together during her lengthy hospital stay.

Humor is also beneficial in times of bereavement, as a way of helping people to deal with the emotional pain in the loss of a dear loved one. I vividly recall one such instance. Upon responding to a call in ICU that a patient had just died, I found a family of four people, the husband and three adult children, of an elderly woman. After introducing myself and expressing my profound sympathy for their loss, I ministered to the family as a group and individually.

Some time later, I began to sense that the children were seriously concerned that their father was experiencing uncontrollable deep vocal grief. All eyes focused on me, as if to say, "Can you help comfort him?" I walked over to Mr. S. who was standing by the bed of his dear wife, put my arm around his shoulder, and said: "Tell me about your life with Mrs. S. How long have you been married?" He responded with "56 years." "That's longer than I am old," I said. A smile came across his face. "I want to hear about the wedding. Did you go on a honeymoon?" Mr. S. said: "I don't remember." "You don't remember? Well, did you have a good time?" "Oh yeah," he responded. "We had a good time!" At that point, we all began to laugh.

For the better part of an hour I listened to stories from Mr. S. and the children about life with their loved one. It was

> *"Those who do not know how to weep with the heart do not know how to laugh either."*
>
> Golda Meir

humor, though, that set the stage for that meaningful time of sharing - therapeutic for all present. Before leaving, I encouraged each person individually to keep those memories alive and fresh. I also shared with them that it is okay and necessary to grieve and express the full range of emotions that accompanies the loss of a loved one.

Another instance of humor being used at a memorial service was recorded in the January 1, 2000 edition of *the Kansas City Star*. In an article entitled "Wilt Remembered," the reporter related in brief some happenings at the funeral service of NBA Hall-of-Famer Wilt Chamberlain, who died in October 1999.

> *"A steady stream of former NBA greats and solemn faces entered Rev. O.C. Smith's religious edifice before the 10 a.m. service started. Ninety minutes later, after the service concluded, the only solemn faces were worn by mourners who were in pain from laughing too hard, or were upset that the service ended too soon."*

On August 6, 1998, I had the honor, along with my brother, of conducting the funeral service for my father. As you might expect by now, I used humor: telling jokes and funny stories. People laughed and cried during the service. Was it easy for me to preach his memorial service? Of course not. I was hurting deeply for Lloyd Jeffers was not only my father but also a dear friend, counselor, source of encouragement and strength – my hero. Humor, though, helped me, my family, and a host of friends deal with the pain of such a significant loss. In fact, one gentleman called me on the phone several hours after the funeral and said: "I don't really know how to say what I want to say so I'll just say it. I can't ever remember going to a funeral that I enjoyed like this one." I knew what he meant; no explanation was needed.

Humor most definitely has a place in ministry to the bereaved.

> *"Why can't we treat death with a certain amount of humanity, dignity, decency, and God forbid, maybe even humor."*
>
> Robin Williams as Patch Adams
> from the movie by the same name

In conclusion, humor appropriately applied in ministry situations with the sick, dying, and bereaved is not to be "humor for the sake of humor" (most especially not sarcastic humor), but humor that evolves from a heart of genuine caring for and empathy with the suffering with the goal of improving quality of life. Humor, with love as the ultimate motivation, can facilitate healing from pain and suffering, and thus, bring about the restoration of inner peace and joy as the way of life.

However, I think it is important to say that the use of humor in ministry is not for everyone. Humor is a gift, a way with people not possessed by everyone. If, though, you do have the gift or even a semblance thereof, cultivate it and use it for empathy is not only crying with the suffering but enabling them to laugh. Lastly, I am sure you have noticed that there are several quotes in this section, as elsewhere in this manual, from the movie *Patch Adams*. While it was very entertaining, to say the least, it is a movie that speaks volumes even for the pastoral care provider about **whole person care**. I highly recommend it for your viewing pleasure with the goal in mind of improving your skills in ministry to those who are suffering.

> *"May the flames of humor, compassion, and love grow in patient care."*

*Contributions by the author.

Medicate the Patient

(Buddhist)

Physicians prescribe medications to begin and continue the healing processes of the body and mind. The clergy should also prescribe spiritual remedies to begin and continue the healing process.

"With my sound spirit, I will build a sound body."

Take daily as needed. Refills: Unlimited

"Illness awakens a great seeking spirit."

Take daily as needed. Refills: Unlimited

"From illness arises the mind that seeks the way."

Take daily as needed. Refills: Unlimited

"Life is inherently endowed with the marvelous capacity to convert even the negative into something positive."

Take morning, noon, and evening. Refills: Unlimited

"Illness is an opportunity for us to attain a higher, nobler state of life."

Take daily as needed. Refills: Unlimited

* Materials adapted from the content of Midwest Bioethics Center's October, 1996, symposium entitled "Religious Diversity and Health Care Treatment Decisions."

Medicate the Patient

(Christian)

Spiritual remedies to facilitate the healing of Christian patients:

"Come to Me all who are growing weary and burdened by a heavy load, and I will give you rest."

Take daily as needed.   Refills: Unlimited

"The Lord is your Keeper... He will neither slumber nor sleep."

Take before bedtime.   Refills: Unlimited

"Be still and know that I am God."

Take morning, noon, and evening.   Refills: Unlimited

"God is a very present help in time of trouble."

Take daily as needed.   Refills: Unlimited

"The Lord is my Shepherd, I shall not want... Even though I walk through the valley of the shadow of death, You are with me; Your rod and staff comfort me."

Take daily as needed.   Refills: Unlimited

* Contributions by the author.

Medicate the Patient

(Hindu)

Spiritual remedies to facilitate the healing of Hindu patients:

"Take refuge in Him alone with all your soul. By His grace will you gain Supreme Peace and Everlasting Abode."

Take morning, noon, and evening.   Refills: Unlimited

"The Maker of all things, self-illumined and all-pervading, He dwells always in the hearts of men."

Take morning, noon, and evening.   Refills: Unlimited

"This (the Self) is the immortal, the fearless. This is Brahman. And of course this Brahman, the name is Satyam, the True."

Take daily as needed.   Refills: Unlimited

"Fix your mind on Me alone, rest your thoughts on Me alone, and in Me alone you will lie hereafter. Of this there is no doubt."

Take daily as needed.   Refills: Unlimited

"This doubt of mine, O Krishna, Thou shouldst completely dispel; for there is none but Thee who can dispel this doubt"

Take daily as needed.   Refills: Unlimited

* Contributions by Anand Bhattacharyya, former president of Hindu Temple and Cultural Center of Kansas City.

Medicate the Patient

(Islamic)

Spiritual remedies to facilitate the healing of Islamic patients.

"All praises are due to Allah, Creator and Sustainer of the Universe."

Take morning, noon, and evening.   Refills: Unlimited

"It is He who guides me... when I am ill, it is He who cures me."

Take daily as needed.   Refills: Unlimited

"This, O God is my prayer. Thine it is to hear. This is my yearning. On Thee is all my reliance."

Take morning, noon, and evening.   Refills: Unlimited

"O Allah! Grant health to my body, to my hearing and to my sight (repeat three times)."

Take daily as needed.   Refills: Unlimited

"In the name of Allah! I seek refuge in Allah's might from the evil of this pain."

Take daily as needed.   Refills: Unlimited

* Contributions by A. Rauf Mir, M.D.

Medicate the Patient

(Jewish)

Spiritual remedies to facilitate the healing of Jewish patients:

"I lift my eyes to the mountains; what is the source of my help? My help comes from A-donai maker of heaven and earth."

Take daily as needed.   Refills: Unlimited

"Into Your hands I entrust my spirit at my time of sleep, and when I awake, and if my spirit is troubled, I shall not fear, for G-d is with me."

Take before bedtime.   Refills: Unlimited

"Send relief and healing for all our diseases, our sufferings and our wounds; for You are a merciful and faithful healer. Blessed are You, G-d."

Take daily as needed.   Refills: Unlimited

"G-d, we're not alone, ever... we always have You!"

Take at all times.   Refills: Unlimited

* Materials adapted from *Circle of Healing: Daily Prayers for Patients, Family and Friends*, submitted by Rabbi Nathan Goldberg, Jewish Community Chaplain, Greater Kansas City Area.

Medicate the Patient

(Native American)

Spiritual remedies to facilitate the healing of Native American patients:

"First thing upon awakening, give thanks to Creator for this day, and before the night is through. Give thanks again for all He has brought to you."

Take morning and evening.   Refills: Unlimited

"Remember, you are not alone. Within every problem there is a gift. All your relations, visible and invisible are with you, holding you in the light of Spirit."

Take daily as needed.   Refills: Unlimited

"As we heal, we become more conscious. As we learn compassion for ourselves, we remember who we really are."

Take morning, noon, and evening.   Refills: Unlimited

"Listen to and follow the guidance given to your heart. Expect guidance to come in many forms: in prayer, in dreams, in solitude and in the words and actions of elders and friends."

Take morning, noon, and evening.   Refills: Unlimited

* Contributions by Rev. Kara Hawkins.

Medicate the Patient

(Unitarian Universalist)

Spiritual remedies to facilitate the healing of Unitarian Universalist patients:

"God is certainly by the bedside of those who suffer, suffering with them, loving them, certainly not condemning them, not compounding the pain."

Take daily as needed.   Refills: Unlimited

"Only one response can maintain us: gratefulness for witnessing the wonder, even amidst life's pain... Be grateful."

Take morning, noon, and evening.   Refills: Unlimited

"Silence creates possibility – the possibility of the word and the song... In silence we rest as the child rests in its mother's arms and we are fed as the child nurses at its mother's breasts."

Take morning, noon, and evening.   Refills: Unlimited

"Praying to God becomes God within, praying in us, close to us at all times offering support and encouragement."

Take morning, noon, and evening.   Refills: Unlimited

* Content for this section was adapted from material provided by Rev. David A. Johnson, pastor of Shawnee Mission Unitarian Universalist Church, Shawnee Mission, Kansas.

A Sample Prescription Form

(Buddhist)

```
         Medicine Buddhas Health Clinic
     Buddha Bhaisajyaguru, Master of Remedies
              Impermanence Avenue
                 Nirvana 88888
Phone: Sutra 8000

Office Hours: 24 hours a day              DEA #4
```

Name:_____ Date:_____

Address:_____

℞

Dr._____ Dr._____

Substitution Permitted   Dispense as Written

Refills: Unlimited

This "Sample Prescription Form" and those which follow are only for the purpose of illustrating one way of "medicating the patient" with spiritual remedies. However, a word of caution is in order before using such a form in your ministry to the sick. Ask yourself: "Will the use of this or any other method of this nature be considered as offensive or trite to patients?" Be thoughtful in your contemplation. Then, if after giving the issue serious consideration, you feel that this form would be helpful and enhance your ministry, use it; adapt it to reflect your own faith tradition. I offer this as simply a suggestion and to arouse your own sense of creativity (the author).

* Contributions by Lama Chuck Stanford and the author.

A Sample Prescription Form

(Christian)

```
                    Whole Health Clinic
              Jesus The Great Physician, M.D.
                   10 Gold Street, Suite
                       Heaven 77777
Phone: Jeremiah 33:3

Office Hours: 24 hours a day                    DEA #12
```

Name:_____ Date:_____

Address:_____

℞

Dr._____   Dr._____

Substitution Permitted   Dispense as Written

Refills: Unlimited

* Contributions by the author.

A Sample Prescription Form

(Hindu)

```
              Hindu Health Clinic
           Krishna, The Great Healer
              Immortal Boulevard
                 Heaven 00108
Phone: Gita VIII 14-15

Office Hours: 24 hours a day                    DEA #108
```

Name:_____ Date:_____

Address:_____

℞

Dr._____   Dr._____

Substitution Permitted   Dispense as Written

Refills: Unlimited

* Contributions by Anand Bhattacharyya.

A Sample Prescription Form

(Jewish)

```
           Shalom Whole Health Clinic
            G-d, The Eternal Healer
              Omnipotent Avenue
               Everywhere 00613
Phone: Jeremiah 33:3

Office Hours: 24 hours a day              DEA #18
```

Name:_____ Date:_____

Address:_____

℞

Dr._____ Dr._____
Substitution Permitted   Dispense as Written

Refills: Unlimited

---

* Submitted by Nina Shik, RN, MSN, CIC, Clinical Nurse Specialist, Shawnee Mission Medical Center, Shawnee Mission, Kansas.

A Sample Prescription Form

(Native American)

Spirit Before Me
Spirit Behind Me
Spirit to the Left and Right of Me
Spirit Above and Below Me

Phone: 24 hours a day

Office Hours: Sunrise to Sunrise   DEA #7

Name:_____   Date:_____

Address:_____

Rx

Dr._____   Dr._____

Substitution Permitted   Dispense as Written

Refills: Unlimited

* Contributions by Rev. Kara Hawkins.

A Decalogue for Those Who Care for the Seriously Ill

Thou Shalt Not

- **Be afraid to touch.** Touching is one of the most comforting modes of communication. A squeeze of the hand or a warm embrace eloquently testifies to how much you truly care.

- **Hesitate to smile and laugh**, not with forced frivolity but with the sheer enjoyment of humorous incidents and stories. Serious illness does not put a ban on laughter.

- **Be uncomfortable with silence.** Love understands love; it needs no words. Silence can be as supportive as shared conversation.

- **Offer untrue statements.** When a patient may be doing poorly, do not say: "You're doing so well." "There's nothing seriously wrong." "You'll soon be as good as new." Everyone should be treated with dignity and respect.

- **Believe you need to have all the answers** and solve all the problems. Just listen, and hear what is said. There are times when there are no complete solutions. Accept your own limited self and commit yourself only to what you are about to do.

Thou Shalt

- **Accept the feelings of the sick person.** Do not pretend that everything is okay. An ill person needs to express his or her emotions. You can encourage that individual by saying: "What are you feeling?" "Tell me what's happening to you." "It must be very hard." Be sensitive to shifting feelings, whether they be sadness, rage, panic, or frustration.

- **Share time together.** Talking, listening to music, watching television, playing games can help fill lonely and frightening hours with shared companionship.

- **Offer to help.** "I'm going to the supermarket. Can I pick up something for you?" "I'll take your kids to the school picnic."

"While the nurse is away this afternoon, I'll come over to the house." Actions do often speak louder than words.

- ❖ **Locate other support.** There may be many people and organizations that can offer invaluable assistance – family, friends, church, synagogue, temple, mosque, home health care, self-help groups, medical organizations. These vital people and groups can help to better manage the difficult moments for both patient and significant other.

- ❖ **Respect the privacy and integrity of the sick person.** If possible, call before you make a home visit. You might inquire: "Do you feel like company this morning?" Never assume you know what the person's needs may be at any given moment. <u>And always, always keep knowledge of the patient confidential</u>.

* Materials adapted from *In Sickness and In Health* by Dr. Earl Grollman.

Ministry Needs for the Seriously Ill: A Patient's Perspective

Concerned people who want to help **the chronically ill and their families** can do so, Doyle and Pat Roberts maintain. The former Missourians indicate that an attitude of sincerity and willingness to give of one's time and energy are appreciated by people suffering from lingering illnesses.

In learning to deal with Roberts' own kidney dysfunction, the couple has discovered inroads to ministering to the chronically ill.

Following are their lists of advice for people who want to help, as well as comments from three pastoral care ministers who are experts on ministering to the ill. They are: J. Thomas Meigs, Minister of Pastoral Care and Wellness at Park Cities Baptist Church, Dallas; Dale Wright, chaplain at Baptist Medical Center, Kansas City; and Jim Lockhart, chaplain at Missouri Baptist Hospital, St. Louis.

Attitude

- Be a friend – in good times and bad.
- Discuss the illness with the patient and family – let them talk.
- Allow them the freedom to express fears about the future, or even death.
- Treat them like "normal" people.
- Give sympathy and understanding, not pity.
- A physical problem affects the entire family.
- A chronic illness results in unpredictable times of alternating good and bad health.

Dr. Meigs agrees with the major thrust of what the Roberts are saying in this list. *"They are letting people know what they have found to be helpful in their experience,"* he said. *"Often, friends will sincerely want to help a chronically ill person, but they really don't know what to do so they back off,"* Meigs continued. *"When that happens, the patient gets on the defensive. The best way to help is to listen to the patient and let them set the agenda,"* he said.

Chaplain Wright agreed that it is good to let the patients talk freely about their feelings. *"If you're always trying to buoy them up and be cheerful, you aren't giving them a chance to talk about their fears,"* he explained. *"If a negative matter is on the patient's mind, let him talk about it. If he wants to talk about depression or the progress of the disease, don't back away from it. Let those people know that you will go as deep as they want to go in talking about their feelings,"* he added. *"Meet the patients where they are."*

Chaplain Lockhart noted he would underscore the sixth point on the 'attitude' list.

"Remember the patient's family with ministry and concern," he said. *"When you call to check on the patient's status, talk to the family about their feelings, too. Include them in your effort to be helpful and supportive."*

Keep in Touch

- Make a phone call – when the patient is well and when he or she is not.

- Make a home visit – especially when the patient is better and can enjoy your company.

- Make a hospital visit – make it short and cheerful.

- Include the hospital patient in conversation with the family and friends present in the room.

- Send cards anytime – not just when the patient is hospitalized. Include the family; give a scripture verse.

- Give a gift – be careful, though, about foods that may be prohibited.

- Invite the family for a meal when the patient is hospitalized, or take a prepared dish.

- Sit with the patient to give the family a break to relax.

- If you offer to help, be willing to honor a request.

- Tell the family you are praying that God will comfort and strengthen them; then be sure to honor that promise.

Meigs emphasized keeping promises to a chronically ill person. *"If you say you'll keep in touch, then do so,"* he urged. *"People in situations like this are more mindful of time than we are. If you say you'll call 'tomorrow,' they'll be expecting you to call 'tomorrow.'"*

Concerning personal visits, Wright said, *"People often wonder how frequently they should visit, and how often a visit is effective and reasonable. Don't give up and forget about the person. Ask them or their family when would be the best time to visit, how often to come and for how long."*

Lockhart added that a phone call to see if the patient is up to a visit is a good idea. He also said to include personal notes in cards. *"Don't just sign your name." "Additionally, a gift is appropriate when the relationship with the patient is close,"* he said. *"But don't just feel like you have to bring a gift every time you visit someone who is ill. The gift of yourself – your visit and conversation – is more beneficial."*

Don'ts

- Do not judge health by appearance.

- Do not ask the family to call you about a doctor's visit; you call them.

- Do not say you understand or know just how they feel, if you have not had a similar experience.

- Do not ask how they are unless you are willing to listen.

- Do not condemn the patient's activities – encourage them.

- Do not ask the family if the hospitalization is the "same old thing." Each hospitalization creates its own fears and needs.

- Do not whisper in the patient's presence. He or she may wonder what bad news you are withholding.

Meigs noted this list continues to emphasize the need to listen to the patient. He pointed out, *"You may not know how they feel, but you can listen with sincere concern and try to understand what they are going through."*

Chaplain Lockhart said the last point is important for any patient, whether they are experiencing a long-term or short-term illness. *"Never whisper in front of a patient,"* he emphasized. *"If you want to talk privately to a family member, do it in a waiting room. And don't ask a family member to leave the patient's room so you can talk; that's just as bad. The patient will think you're keeping something from him."*

Chaplain Wright said the three lists are all valid and contain good advice. *"Overall,"* he said, *"it is important not to forget the patient over the long haul. Chronically ill patients face many lonely days. Your contact with them is important, whether it is weekly or monthly. Don't forget them!"*

> *"Treat a disease: you win, you lose;*
> *Treat a person: you win no matter what the outcome."*
>
> Robin Williams as Patch Adams
> from the movie by the same name

* Adapted from the article, "Aiding the Ill: Checklists for Concerned Christians" that appeared in the *Word and Way*, the Missouri state paper of Southern Baptists.

Do You Know What Hope Is?

It's magic and it's free.
It's not in a prescription,
It's not in an IV.
It punctuates our laughter,
It sparkles in our tears.
It simmers under sorrows,
And dissipates our fears.

Do you know what Hope is?
It's reaching past today,
It's dreaming of tomorrow,
It's trying a new way.
It's pushing past Impossible,
It's pounding on the door.
It's questioning the Answers,
It's always seeking more.
It's rumors of a breath,
It's whispers of a cure.
A roller coaster ride
Of remedies unsure.

Do you know what Hope is?
It's candy for the soul,
It's perfume for the spirit,
To share it, makes it whole.

~Author Unknown

Hope: A Timeless Treasure

Hope is a powerful ingredient in the holistic healing process. "It is a balm of comfort from the past; it is an assurance that God will bless us in the present; it is an assurance that relief and good are provided for our future."

> *"When you have religious faith, you live with constant reminders of hope."*
>
> Harold Koenig, M.D.

Hope as Past Experience

Many people have a personal history of what God has done for them or someone close to them, as well as what God has done in the broader context of religious history. This faith history validates hope as a substantive reality and provides the opportunity for intervention into the lives of those needing help and encouragement. Faith itself reasons that God, who was faithful in the past, will continue to be faithful. Thus, the person of faith can count upon God's wisdom, love, power, grace, and mercy to work out the best in the current difficult situation.

Hope as Future Experience

Hope understood in this sense enables many sufferers to look forward to a better tomorrow in this world. This hope has a practical consequence; it helps the suffering one compare the current experience with the desired future experience. Additionally, the concept of hope as future experience can enable one to mobilize personal resources for self-help and have a receptive attitude to help from God and others. This concept of hope can also cause one to look forward to a better world than the present one.

Hope as Present Experience

This rendition of hope tells us that the present is not permanent. The power of hope as present experience is found in an interpersonal process:

> *"True hoping requires an inter-personal context... Isolation leads to hopelessness and to disintegration of personality functioning. When communication between persons fails, the isolated individual goes to pieces... who gives hope to whom is an irrelevant question; the point is that hoping is generated in the relationship."*
>
> Paul Pruyser, Ph.D.

The present experience of hope happens through the minister "helper." The helper can:

❖ Enable the patients to accept themselves as they are by assuring them that others accept them.

❖ Explore with patients the matter of personal goals and purposes for living.

❖ Point out the presence of God with suffering people.

❖ Facilitate the mobilization of resources for patients: both personal and extended (i.e. family and friends).

❖ Attempt to answer religious and philosophical questions.

❖ Be a catalyst for a positive attitude in the midst of difficulty.

❖ Represent the concern of the faith community.

This "Ministry of Hope:"

- ❖ Is always possible.

- ❖ Can be reinforced.

- ❖ Keeps people going in tough times.

> *"I want to connect with people, to offer counsel and hope."*
>
> Robin Williams as Patch Adams
> from the movie by the same name

---

* Adapted from materials contained in *Lay Shepherding* by Rudolph E. Grantham along with contributions by the author.

Hope-Inspiring Strategies

- ❖ Project joy.
- ❖ Relate that setbacks are often only temporary.
- ❖ Focus on spirituality.
- ❖ Center attention on what the patient <u>can</u> do.
- ❖ Comfort often.
- ❖ Care always.
- ❖ Communicate positive messages.
    - God is good.
    - You are lovable.
    - You are loved.
    - You are not forgotten.
    - You are in community.

> *"One little ray of hope in a world of darkness is enough to invigorate some people."*
>
> Paul Pruyser, Ph.D.

* Adapted from materials submitted by Mark Fenton and the author.

Talking with Sick People

Talking with sick people, especially patients in a hospital, creates anxiety for some individuals. They are aware that the sick person is more vulnerable and sensitive. They may be afraid they will say something that will hurt the patient or cause the condition to get worse. Often, they just do not know what to say because they are not sure what the sick person is experiencing.

What you say to patients and how you say it will be determined by where they are in the process of illness. You should have little to say to patients immediately after serious surgery; you should have more to say to them during the long hours of convalescence. However, before you do much talking, it will be important for you to do much listening, that is, if the patient has a need and desire to talk. Furthermore, nonverbals during these times of illness often say more than any words patients might utter. Therefore, listen carefully as well to what is not said. Sometimes patients may not have much energy, and talking will be a real chore for them. In such instances, it will be better for you to have some well-chosen words of encouragement. Of course, where appropriate offering a prayer for patients can also be helpful.

> "Rather than speaking so people will listen, listen so people will speak."
>
> Dave Hiller, Ph.D., Emory University

Generally speaking, one should carefully listen to patients to understand the feelings, needs and concerns being experienced. Keep in mind, though, that the effects of disease as well as of medication may cause patients to distort or misinterpret what is going on around them. Therefore, do not always assume that what patients are saying is true. For example, they may indicate that their doctor has not been in to see them or has not communicated anything about their medical condition. The facts may be that both of these things have happened, but the patients do not remember or may not want to remember, especially if what was related was unpleasant or threatening.

Our own anxiety sometimes causes us to say things to patients which are inappropriate or harmful. For example: "What's wrong with you?" or

"How did the enema go?" Instead, try: "How is the day going for you?" or "Has it been the kind of day you had hoped for?" Furthermore, try to keep a balance between being too cheerful and too somber. People in pain may be repulsed by someone who bubbles with forced frivolity in an effort to "cheer them up." Patients may see this as artificial and resent your insensitivity. On the other hand, avoid a funereal look and attitude. If your approach is as if you are ready to bury them, you may frighten them and certainly lower their morale and sense of hope.

You will also want to avoid prematurely or falsely reassuring patients about their situation. Be careful about sharing experiences you or "friends" have had with illness. Patients sometime read into what others say what they want to hear or may be afraid of hearing. People experience illness in ways that are unique to them, and your experiences with the same illness may not necessarily be akin to theirs. At the same time, patients may be helped to know that because of your experience with illness you know something of what they are going through and feeling.

Do not try to answer questions which only doctors and nurses have authority to answer. Refer the patient to these persons. Be alert to ways in which you can reinforce patients' confidence in the people who are caring for them and patients' capacity to trust those professionals, themselves, and, ultimately, God. This confidence will be an important ingredient in making the treatment program effective.

If patients express a good deal of guilt feeling, encourage them to talk about such matters. If you have experienced God's forgiveness and acceptance, you might witness to this as a way of reminding patients that such is available to them, also.

Finally, hear the patients out as to their hopes and fears; provide encouragement;

"Look to this day
For yesterday is but a dream,
And tomorrow is only a vision,
But today, well lived,
Makes every yesterday a dream of happiness,
And every tomorrow a vision of hope.
Look well, therefore, to this day."

Sanskrit proverb submitted by
Lama Chuck Stanford

assure them of your prayerful concern; and if you can, offer confidence in them and in those who are caring for them. Let patients know that there are those who are praying for them and concerned about them. Above all, remind them of God's faithfulness not to abandon them in their infirmities but to be present with them in their trouble; for where God is, there is hope. Because of that fact, it would be most beneficial if you could in some way enable the patient to adopt the attitude reflected in this poem.

---

* Adapted from materials by Dr. John H. Boyle, former Professor of Pastoral Counseling at Southern Baptist Theological Seminary and former CPE Supervisor and Chaplain at University Hospital, both in Louisville, Kentucky along with commentary from J. Thomas Meigs and the author.

Listening: A Balm for Healing

> *"You are an easy person to talk to."*

What is it that makes a person easy to talk to? Is it a genetically transmitted trait? Is it related to one's personality type? Is it a learned behavior? Perhaps, the latter of these is the most relevant for discussion because, according to one pastoral care professional, it is awareness or knowledge and appropriation of the parts of the communication process that facilitate listening which heals.

Major Components of Communication

- ❖ **Word symbols** – words are the most obvious, but not necessarily the most important, part of communication. They do not contain the entire message; they may even be intended to hide the real message. Therefore, the question of what do the words convey by way of facts and/or feelings needs to be considered by a "listening healer." Words may convey intellectual content alone without any emotion. On the other hand, words may reveal the emotions of the speaker.

- ❖ **Nonverbal symbols** – These elements of the communication process project rational as well as emotional messages. A person does not have to utter a sound, and an astute observer can detect anger, guilt, gratitude as communicated through such things as facial expressions, color changes in skin tone, overall demeanor. Body language, the way one dresses, certain mannerisms can also communicate a powerful message. In fact, nonverbal symbols can, and often do, speak louder and with greater clarity than words.

- ❖ **Silence** – This is closely related to nonverbal symbols, but is not synonymous, and hence, deserves to be treated separately. Silence can connote meaningful nonverbal communication: thoughtful contemplation, fear, grief. In such cases, "words can not only be irrelevant, but irreverent." On the other hand, silence can simply reveal a "mind out of gear." It can also be used to conceal something which a person does not wish to share. Furthermore, silence can be a way of withdrawal from something or someone that causes discomfort.

Principles of Listening That Heal

❖ This type of communication causes the listener to be in empathy with the speaker by focusing upon what appears to have the most meaning and importance to the speaker. Active listening involves more than the ears; it involves the eyes, mouth, memory, and feelings as the following concepts relate.

❖ **Concentrate upon the speaker** – Listen with the "inner ear" to the words and nonverbal symbols to enhance the "outer ear's" ability to hear with heightened clarity.

❖ **Reflect to the person what you heard** – Use questions like "Did I understand you to say...?" or "Did I detect some anxiety in your voice?" This gives the speaker the opportunity to correct your failure to hear correctly or to amplify further if your perceptions were accurate.

❖ **Ask for clarification of details** – This is important if you are unable to follow confused words or feelings. This technique also suggests to the speaker that you are genuinely interested and desire to understand.

❖ **Summarize what you have heard** – Summarization serves the purpose of bringing order to the conversation and provides the impetus for the speaker to elaborate further on the issue(s).

"Conversation may be sacrament, for through it and the feeling it sets into play, the grace of God flows through you into another."

Roadblocks to Effective Listening

❖ **Language itself** – The same words may have different meanings for different people. Additionally, some feelings and experiences are hard to express in words.

❖ **Listener preoccupation with something else** – This happens to almost everyone. When such does occur, it is difficult to focus on the speaker's situation.

❖ **Listener impatience** – There are multiple reasons why this might happen: wordy speaker who rambles; speaker's inability to express with clarity; speaker's non-allowance for feedback.

❖ **Listener condemnation** – Condescending judgment may well silence the speaker because he or she cannot or will not tolerate that type of treatment. By the way, this is contrary to the method and purpose of a "listening healer."

❖ **Listener argumentation** – The problem here is usually with the listener who refuses to listen to and/or who challenges an opinion other than his or her own. Whatever the reason for listener arguing, the result is "alienation."

❖ Roadblocks, though, do naturally occur in communication. Therefore, they must be recognized, admitted, and dealt with in the best way possible. Other roadblocks to the "healing listener" that deserve special mention are:

- Fear of being changed
- Fear of close relationships
- Fear of silence
- Differences in gender communication patterns
- Distractions
- Interruptions
- Premature giving of advice

* Adapted from a chapter entitled "Listening that Develops Wholeness" in *Lay Shepherding* by Rudolph E. Grantham, *How to Make Pastoral Calls* by Russell L. Dicks and contributions by the author.

More Tips on Listening as a Vital Component of Effective Ministry

> *"Listening to another person and giving them your full attention is one of the greatest gifts you can give."*

Since listening is "a balm for healing," its importance cannot be minimized or even overstated. Allen Ivey as the central maxim of his book *Basic Attending Skills* poignantly reflects the truth of that statement.

> *Listen, listen, listen, and then listen some more before taking action or giving advice."*

The information that follows is a synopsis of six essential skills for effective listening.

- ❖ **Attending Behavior** – Ivey deems this as the "foundation of effective listening." He suggests four key dimensions of this listening skill.

    1. **Eye Contact** – How important is this? Consider the following: We hear with our ears, but we <u>listen</u> with our ears and our eyes. "Granddaddy, I like it when you listen to me with your eyes." Look at the person to whom you are talking. However, do not stare. Be aware also that breaks in eye contact are normal. The same can be instrumental to the helper and helpee as to where the other is in the process. Incidentally, it is important to remember that differing cultures view eye contact differently. For example, African Americans and Native Americans, among other groups, may view maintained eye contact as a sign of

disrespect. Nevertheless, eye contact (and when to avoid it) is an important tool in effective listening.

2. **Attentive Body Language** – It has been suggested by some researchers that 85 percent of communication is nonverbal. Whether you realize it or not, your posture connotes listening or non-listening, interest or disinterest. In our culture, a slight forward trunk lean indicates one is listening. It is important, though, to not appear forced into a body position that is unnatural to you. Find your own style of comfort. Be conscious of your body position and movements and how they project to the other that you are an attentive, interested, comfortable listener.

3. **Vocal Style** – Volume, tone of voice, rate of speech often indicate interest or disinterest. Our feelings about things are not only reflected by eye contact or body language, but through our voices. [A danger, though, in making a judgment regarding another's interest or dis-interest based on vocal style in what you are sharing is that you compare his or her vocal style with that of your own (i.e. how you are feeling about something reflected by your own vocal style).] Use your natural voice that communicates your emotions. As with eye contact and body language, vocal style can vary from group to group.

4. **Verbal Following** – Stay on the topic. Take your cues for conversation from the one to whom you are listening. Ask questions or make comments about the topic of discussion.

❖ **Open Invitation To Talk** – The first task of the pastoral visitor is "to stay out of the patient's way" so as to find out how the patient sees the situation and defines the issues. A way to accomplish that task is to provide limited structure through the use of questions that are of two types: open and closed.

Both open and closed questions can be of five different types:

1. Cognitive
2. Emotional
3. Social
4. Theological
5. Spiritual

Similarly, both open and closed questions can be used to address any of the differing types of questions as noted above:

- What would you like to know about your illness? *(Cognitive/Open)*
- Do you understand what the doctor said? *(Cognitive/Closed)*
- What are some of your worries? *(Emotional/Open)*
- Illness often causes fears. Has this been true for you? *(Emotional/Closed)*
- Have you felt isolated or alone during your illness? *(Social/Closed)*
- What kind of support network do you have? *(Social/Open)*
- How has this illness affected your view of God? *(Theological/Open)*
- Where do you think God is? *(Theological/Closed)*
- Where do you get your strength during times like these? *(Spiritual/Open)*
- Has this illness caused you to question the meaning of life? *(Spiritual/Closed)*

(Even though there is a close relationship between theological and spiritual, they are not identical in meaning. Theological has more to do with "what a person thinks about God" – intellectual. Spiritual, on the other hand, focuses on "how one relates to God" – experiential.)

Both types of questions are useful, but open questions can make for a more meaningful pastoral visit because they are reflexive, lead to self-discovery, useful information gatherers, and discussion enhancers. Additionally, open questions are more helpful for the following reasons:

- They can help begin and keep a conversation going.

- They enable the patient to elaborate as opposed to a "few-words answer."

- They provide the opportunity to elicit specific behaviors so the pastoral visitor is more readily able to understand what and how the patient is feeling.

Finally, how to phrase questions is of utmost importance in being an effective helper listener. *"What," "How," "Could"* are usually the three best words to use in forming the interrogative.

1. Could questions – give control of the conversation to the patient and establish trust with the questioner. "Could you give me an example?"

2. What questions – lead the helper to talk about specifics uncovered in the "could" questions. "What does that mean to you?"

3. How questions – can enable the patient to talk about process or emotions. "How do you feel about that?"

❖ **Minimal Encourage** – These are small verbal and nonverbal indicators to patients that you are with and following them in the conversation. Nonverbal "minimal encourages" are things likes head nods, leaning your body forward to indicate interest, open gestures with the hands. Verbal "minimal encourages" are short utterances, maybe even "grunts," for the express purpose of helping the patient move on and deeper into the conversation:

- "Oh?" "And?" "So?"

- "Uh-huh." "Ummm."

- "Help me understand that."

- "Tell me more!"

- Repetition of one or more key words – "Going home?" "You think/feel…?"

Repetition is a very important type of "minimal encourage." When key words or short phrases are restated, the patient will usually respond by elaborating on the concept in more detail.

❖ **Paraphrase** – This attending skill is an amplification of the minimal encourage. The value of the paraphrase is that it lets the patients know that you have truly heard what they said. An example of the distinction between minimal encourage and paraphrase is as follows:

- "Going home?" -- *minimal encourage*

- "Jim, you said that if the results of the test come back negative, the doctor is going to send you home and treat the condition with medication. Is that correct?" -- *paraphrase*

You will notice the question at the conclusion of the paraphrase. We call that the "check-out." By using this technique, you are checking the accuracy of your hearing and, at the same time, "keeping the ball in the court of the patient" who can correct any misunderstanding before proceeding further into the conversation. Paraphrasing at certain points can facilitate movement to a new or different subject if the issue has been exhausted. One important thing to keep in mind: paraphrase is not interpretation.

> *"… If you listen first, many patients will come to useful and correct interpretations on their own."*

- **Reflection of Feeling** – Words spoken are the content portion of the communication. <u>How</u> the patient shares will reflect the feelings experienced. Pastoral response to the feelings being expressed can help the patient move toward a more complete understanding of the situation. There are several helpful things one can do in reflecting feelings.

   - Name the feelings through use of actual word, metaphor or description of nonverbal communication.

   - Use a sentence structure like "You seem to feel…" or "I sense you are feeling…" and add the named emotion, as you perceive it.

   - If not certain of the feeling expressed, add a "check-out:" … "Is that the way you feel?"

   A relationship of trust is essential, in most situations, before patients will share their feelings. However, even if there is such a relationship, some patients will find it difficult to share and explore their feelings. This is especially true with men who are expected in many cultures to suppress their emotions. If nothing else, at least the acknowledgment of feeling by the pastor will go a long way in communicating to the patient that you genuinely care and understand something of what they are experiencing.

- **Summarization** – The primary purpose of this basic skill is to help the patient bring together into a harmonious whole the behavior, thoughts, and feelings. Secondarily, summarization is a way to check whether or not you as the helper have heard and understood correctly. The distinction between summarization and paraphrase is the period of time involved; the time period covered by a summary is longer than that of a paraphrase. The skill of summarization is most useful when the ministry encounter is broken by a length of time (e.g. from one day to the next), and you as the helper want to continue the conversation of the previous visit. Incidentally, the content of summarization (following the "check out") can often be the prayer or petition presented to God. You might ask the patient: "Can we talk to God about these concerns?"

> *"You can be most helpful if you are truly yourself."*
>
> *"Patients will talk about topics to which you are able and willing to listen."*

Listening is a primary task of the caring minister in order that he or she can understand the patient's point of view and feelings. Effective listening by using these basic skills can facilitate greater under-standing of problems and opportunities for growth and problem solving.

---

* The vast majority of this section was taken from *Basic Attending Skills* by Allen E. Ivey, Norma B. Gluckster and Mary Bradford Ivey. Additional material was extracted from an article entitled "Ministry of Healing" by Chaplain Jerry Rexin. The author also provided comments and suggestions.

A Case Study in Effective Listening

The *"Record of Pastoral Call"* related here is an actual ministry encounter that I experienced. The conversation as written is an accurate reconstruction of the substance of what transpired between the two participants: Chaplain Steve Jeffers and the patient.

My first encounter with the middle-aged female patient was in the Emergency Department at 3:00 AM. The patient was admitted and remained hospitalized for almost two months. This particular visit occurred during the sixth week of her stay in the hospital. My intended plan for the visit was to offer continuing encouragement with respect to her physical, emotional, and spiritual health.

To protect patient confidentiality, the patient's initial has been changed.

As you read the dialogue, I invite you to look carefully for the use of any of the listening/attending skills discussed in the previous section. What would you have done or said in this particular situation? Would your responses and behavior have been similar or different?

P1. (Knocking on the wall as I walk in) Come in.

C1. Hi, B.! How are you doing this morning?

P2. Better than nothing (she laughs). Do you see anything different in here? (I look around the room for a few seconds.)

C2. The balloons in the corner?

P3. Yes, but look, my oxygen is gone! (Pointing to her face)

C3. Boy, that's great! You are improving remarkably well, a definite direct response to the prayers of many people.

P4. I know. Do you remember our conversation a few weeks back when I was in ICU about illness being a spiritual experience? (We had an extended conversation about how illness can help people take a more serious look at life and its meaning in the present, future, and even afterlife. The result of that conversation was B's desire to become more involved in Christian ministry.)

C4. I certainly do. I remember that being a very significant time and turning point in your life.

P5. It was. I've been reading the Bible a lot lately and listening to Christian radio. I have read and heard things that are helping me a lot (she is smiling). As you well know, I have been around churches a lot (she was custodian at a church for 17 years) and got a lot of religion by osmosis.

C5. Osmosis? What do you mean by that?

P6. Well, you get a lot of information – facts.

C6. I see. And facts are not unimportant. But since Christianity is relational, it's important to make a transference of the "osmosis obtained religion" into a personal relationship with God.

P7. You are right. You know there have been several times I have wanted to go forward in church. I felt a voice telling me to and then something inside me says you are not ready.

C7. Go forward?

P8. Yes, to rededicate my life. I have been baptized. (At this time the occupational therapist comes in, stops when she sees me, and I motion her to come on in. I needed to leave right then in order to be able to get to St. Luke's, so this was a good way for me to break off this conversation and pick up where we left off at a later time.)

Therapist 1. (Looking at B.) You are in bed. (Looking at me) I'm not interrupting, am I?

C8. Not at all. B., we'll pick up this discussion tomorrow, okay?

P9. That sounds good. I want to.

C9. So do I. See you tomorrow. (I start walking out.)

P10. Bye, Steve. (I return the next day as I promised to continue the discussion.)

Next Visit

C10. (Knocking on the wall as I walk in) Hi, B. You are looking mighty chipper this morning.

P11. Yes, you know what I did yesterday after you left?

C11. No? Tell me.

P12. Well, I walked twice around the nurses' station. That's over 300 feet.

C12. Great!

P13. I also bathed myself.

C13. You were quite a busy girl. I bet it felt so good to bathe yourself, didn't it?

P14. Oh, yeah. Nobody can do that quite like you can for yourself. (She is smiling so much more this morning than on any previous visit over the last six weeks.)

C14. I agree. It sure is good to see that smile on your face.

P15. I know. I just didn't feel like it before with all the uncertainty and fear about what might happen.

C15. Uh huh. (nodding my head)

P16. I don't have the fear anymore like I'm going to die, but there is still some uncertainty or confusion I feel.

C16. Can you tell me more about that uncertainty and confusion?

P17. It's hard for me to put my finger on. It's inside of me.

C17. Does it have anything to do with our discussion yesterday morning? (I felt that it did for she has never talked with me like that before.)

P18. Yes, it does.

C19. I remember you telling me over a month ago when you were in ICU that this has been a spiritual experience for you, and we talked about that. Do you remember that?

P19. Oh, yes.

C20. Yesterday I remember you mentioning several things: feeling a voice telling you to go forward and another telling you you weren't ready, rededicating your life, and about baptism. Is that correct? (The therapist walks into the room and asks B. if she is busy. She said yes and asked her to come back later if that would be okay. She smiled and said that would be fine.)

P20. Yes, but I've already been baptized.

C21. Okay. Can we talk about some of those other things? (There was silence for a few seconds, which seemed like an eternity. I was tempted to say something but restrained myself thinking that possibly she was trying to formulate what to say.)

P21. When my husband and I got married we agreed we would never have pets. I didn't want to draw close to something and then be hurt when it died or ran away.

C22. Uh huh? (nodding, but wondering where she was going with this)

P22. I usually keep people at arm's length (making gesture with her arm). When I worked for the church all those years, I just did the work. I guess I just walked the walk but didn't do any talking. Now, I'm doing the same thing working at the school. I wonder where I'll be ten years from now.

C23. Do you mean professionally?

P23. No, with the Lord. I've kept Him at arm's length, too. (Tears began to run down her face, and her voice starts to crack.)

C24. How can that be changed?

P24. I guess I need to rededicate my life.

C25. (Smiling) It appears to me that you are in the process of doing that right now.

P25. You think so? (A somewhat surprised look on her face)

C26. I certainly do. These last several weeks have truly been a spiritual journey.

P26. An awakening.

C27. Yes!

P27. I'm normally not an emotional person (attempting to apologize for the tears and cracking voice).

C28. B., I think it is quite normal for people to get emotional about things and people that are of utmost concern and importance. (She smiles as if to say, "I understand.") Let me say something else about rededication; it is not simply a one-time action but an action that needs to be continually repeated in order for the relationship to be kept fresh and vibrant. Constant attention needs to be given to any relationship for it to be intimate and meaningful.

P28. That makes good sense. You know, I feel a peace and calmness that I haven't felt in a long time.

C29. Can you tell me a little more about that?

P29. Well, as I told you, I have been wanting to "go down" for a long time but didn't. I now know that I really want to do a lot of things at church when I get home and feel up to it.

C30. So, you are feeling peace and calmness because of things you are going to do at the church?

P30. Weeell, no because I feel closer to the Lord.

C31. He's not at arm's length anymore?

P31. No.

C32. Would it be safe to say then that the reason for your peace and calmness is because of a more qualitative relationship with the Lord?

P32. Yes! (Smiling)

C33. B., let me share one final thought with you. (The time is close to 9:00 AM, and she told me as our conversation began that a friend from Arkansas was going to call at 9:00 AM. She also asked me to move the phone where she could reach it.) This is something I have shared at my church and try to practice in my own life. A person's priorities should be in this order: God first, family second, and everything else in some type of order beyond these two, and that includes church. I guarantee you that you will be a far better wife, friend, employee, and even church member if the most important thing in your life is to have an intimate relationship with God. With respect to "doing things at church" or even attending church, the most important thing is not that you do things or even attend regularly, but the reason for such. Is it simply duty that motivates us or love for Christ? My wife and I are not the most important person in each other's lives. God is. I do not mind playing second fiddle to Him, nor does she. Our relationship with each other is what it is because of that.

P33. That makes really good sense. This has been an awakening.

C34. I would go even further to suggest this experience has been a watershed event in your life.

P34. I think you are right.

C35. B., I feel privileged and honored that you have shared with me today. I am (I'm stumbling around for the right word.) ecstatic! (She smiles.)

P35. Steve, the main reason I wanted to talk to you is that you are learned, and you can give me some answers.

C36. I appreciate your confidence in me, but as I reflect back on our conversation, I did not give you any answers. I was simply a facilitator, providing an opportunity for you to share your burdens, concerns, and come to draw your own conclusion. All I did was provide some guidance along the way. Do you think I gave you any answers?

P36. (Thinking for a minute) I guess not!

C37. B., as one who is genuinely interested in you, I pledge to provide any answers to questions you might have.

P37. Thanks, Steve. I appreciate that.

C38. It's almost time for your phone call; I think a prayer of thanksgiving is in order, don't you?

P38. I sure do!

C39. Dear Father, how grateful I am for the experience of this morning and for the work you are doing in B.'s life. Encourage her and give her the strength to follow your leadership. Help me to be all that I need to be for her. We praise and thank you. In Jesus' name. Amen. God bless you; I will see you later.

P39. See ya, Steve. (Smiling, I leave the room.)

Pastoral evaluation: B. has been hospitalized for a long time (six weeks) as a very sick woman. It has been my experience that many people in similar situations do focus on spiritual matters and often make bargains with God (i.e. they make promises to God of things they will do for Him if He will heal them). Unfortunately, the commitments they frequently make are not kept when the crises are past. I am not saying that will happen in B.'s case. However, I do believe B. will need encouragement from her pastor and church family, along with a support base in the home for continued maturity in the faith.

> *"I want to listen, really listen to people."*
>
> Robin Williams as Patch Adams
> from the movie by the same name

* Contributions by the author.

Prayer:
An Essential Element
Of Pastoral Care

Quotable Quotes
on the Efficacy of Prayer

"God does everything by prayer and nothing without it."

~ John Wesley

"The Indian (American) believes that eighty percent of all cures must first take place in the mind of the patient, otherwise the physical aids may also fall short."

~ David Villasenor

"The al-Fatiha (opening chapter) is the most important Qur'anic passage... It is an all-inclusive prayer that the Creator has sent for Muslims, and the rest of the Qur'an, the remaining 113 chapters, is Allah's response to the prayer."

~ Syed E. Hasan

"God is the essence of bliss, the fount of eternal joy."

~ Swami Aseshananda

"When we pray, we stop trying to control life and remember we belong."

~ Rachel Naomi Remen, M.D.

"You can trace every great movement of God to a kneeling figure."

~ D. L. Moody

"When you load the Pipe and pray to the Grandfather (Great Mystery), whatever you pray for will come true."

~ John around Him

"Prayer helps give us the strength and insight to change things that can be changed, our hearts for instance, even our lives."

~ Forrest Church

"God certainly listens to prayer if it is sincere."

~ Sri Ramakrishna

"Prayers which cannot be uttered are often prayers which cannot be refused."

~ Charles H. Spurgeon

"We believe that human being's spiritual power through prayer is so strong it decides life on earth."

~ Hopi Chief Dan Evehema

"When I pray beside my fellow Muslims, I feel a special bonding that runs deeper than our mutual religious beliefs (experience during Ramadan)."

~ Marie Hasan

"To pray is to regain a sense of the mystery that animates all beings, the divine margin in all attainments. Prayer is our humble answer to the inconceivable surprise of living."

~ Rabbi Abraham Joshua Heschel

"Man is at his greatest and highest when upon his knee he comes face to face with God."

~ D. Martin Lloyd-Jones

"To cry from the wounded heart, "Oh Lord help me!" is the beginning of authentic prayer."

~ Duke T. Gray

"Just as my body needs water, carbohydrates, protein, and lipids, my mind needs Allah, and the only way to Allah is to pray."

~ Islamic Doctor

"God receives us just as we are and accepts our prayers just as they are. In the same way that a small child cannot draw a bad picture, a child of God cannot offer a bad prayer."

~ Quaker, Richard Foster

"It (the prayer) represents the first attempt of the ordinary human soul to approach God."

~ Swami Bhajanananda

"Never give up on God, who always answers our prayers... Continuing to pray hopefully in the face of profound disappointment seems contrary to human nature. Why should we do it? Because invariably we learn and grow in the process."

~ Jimmy Carter, former President of the United States

"The Indian (American) conception of healing is through divine power... the act of cure is usually accomplished amid song, ceremony and prayer."

~ Natalie Curtis

"Just touching and turning a prayer wheel brings incredible purification and accumulates unbelievable merit."

~ Lama Zopa

"Prayer is talking to God, someone I love."

~ Harold G. Koenig, M.D.

"The language of prayer is the language of lyric poetry."

~ Henry Sloan Coffin

"More things are wrought by prayer than this world dreams of."

~ Alfred, Lord Tennyson

"Prayer does not bring God down to us, but brings us up to Him."

~ Ellen G. White

"People who pray for courage, for strength to bear the unbearable, for the grace to remember what they have left instead of what they have lost, very often find their prayers answered."

~ Rabbi Harold S. Kushner

"Silence is the sea which best bears up our prayers... The practice of silence may be the single most real and helpful thing you do each day."

~ Carl Scovel

"Prayer is the Great Conversation."

~ Dale Matthews, M.D.

"Prayer helps us be warriors, not worriers."

~ Larry Dossey, M.D.

"In the Tsalagi (Cherokee) way of praying, we are not asking for something; all we need is already here in abundance. When we pray we are giving thanks for what is and affirming our intention to manifest what is good for all people."

~ Dhyani Ywahoo

"Do it (prayer) every day for a year – or ten – and you will discover that you are such a different person from what you were that you cannot even recognize that Old Self you left behind."

~ Duke T. Gray

"Prayer is the opening of the heart to God as to a friend."

~ Ellen G. White

"Dear God,

Bless Mommy and Daddy, my dog and pet turtle, Grandma and Grandpa. Oh, by the way, God! Take care of Yourself. If something happens to You, we are all sunk..."

~ Small child overheard by his parents

* Contributions by the author derived from a number of written sources and individuals consulted.

Prayer: A Healer of the Ages

"I wouldn't be here if it weren't for God." "God healed me!" These statements and many others like them are commonplace among people from all walks of life – from the playroom to the boardroom. One exception, though, is from the medical community itself, although that is beginning to change. Renowned clinicians from prestigious institutions have been conducting scientific studies for several years which clearly seem to validate faith and prayer as beneficial elements in the healing processes of critically ill patients. I am speaking of: Dr. Harold Koenig of Duke University School of Medicine, Dr. Dale Matthews of Georgetown University Medical Center, and Dr. Herbert Benson of Harvard University School of Public Health, among others. The news of the positive effects of prayer is becoming more widespread among and acceptable to healthcare clinicians.

A front-page article in the October 25, 1999, edition of *The Kansas City Star* entitled "Power of Prayer Gets Scientific Boost" highlights the continuing study into the area of the relationship between religion and medicine. A research team that included cardiologist, James O'Keefe, several other physicians, a psychologist, a statistician, Chaplain Jerry Kolb, and led by Dr. William Harris conducted a project involving 990 heart patients admitted to Saint Luke's Hospital in Kansas City, Missouri, in order to study the effects of intercessory prayer. The findings of the study, as related in *The Kansas City Star* article, led Dr. Harris to conclude that *"The patients who were prayed for just did better... By better, I mean everything that word means."* Cardiologist, Dr. James O'Keefe, is also cited in the newspaper article: *"I'll admit being a scientist, I was very skeptical. There was no scientific mechanism to explain it. But from my perspective, I can tell you the message of this study is simple, clear and harmless. If you or a loved one are in trouble, medically ill, sick, and you feel so inclined, go ahead and pray. Pray for yourself and your loved ones. This study suggests it might help."*

The wall that has divided medicine and religion for over two hundred years is beginning to crumble. Dr. Mitchell Krucoff, Associate Professor of Medicine and Cardiology at Duke University Medical Center, states that *"This is not fringe stuff anymore,"* speaking of studies like the one conducted at Saint Luke's Hospital. *"This is now of mainstream scientific interest. I definitely think that the appearance of these types of studies in mainstream, peer-reviewed journals is a very exciting indication of where medicine is going in the new millennium."* Dr. Koenig adds: *"This is very significant...* It (the current study) *does not offer irrefutable proof that this is a sure effect. But it does offer evidence on which to build. It provides one more match on the stack of evidence."* (The scientific study on intercessory prayer conducted at Saint Luke's Hospital in Kansas City, Missouri, was published in *The Archives of Internal Medicine*, Volume 159, on pages 2273-2278, October 25, 1999. The title of the article is "A Randomized, Controlled Trial of the Effects of Remote, Intercessory Prayer on Outcomes of Patients Admitted to the Coronary Care Unit.")

Studies of this nature will continue and provide overwhelming evidence that faith, prayer, and religious involvement significantly enhance healing and a general sense of well-being. The time is not yet here when physicians will prescribe prayer in the same manner as an antibiotic or some other type of drug, but it may well be on the horizon. In the interim, the various faith communities must continue doing what they have done for millenniums with remarkable results: Pray.

* Contributions by the author.

Some General Principles for Praying With the Sick

- All prayer is addressed to God.

- The hearing of prayer is a means of grace for the patient.

- A primary purpose in prayer for healing is to help the sick relate to God.

- Prayer should stress the presence, glory, and power of God rather than His gifts.

- Prayer should lift up the spiritual, emotional, social and physical needs of the patient.

- Prayer should (in general) be positive, affirming the patient's faith and strengths.

- Prayer should acknowledge the reality of the many ways God heals emphasizing "not my will, but Thy will be done."

- Prayer should be honest, thereby paving the way for the continuing of God's presence in whatever comes to pass.

- Patients should respond to prayer with commitment to action.

- The "pray-er" is a mediator assisting in a relationship between God and the patient.

* Material for this section was adapted from *Lay Shepherding* by Rudolph E. Grantham along with contributions by the author.

Prayers for Use in Hospital Ministry

The following prayers reflect many of the needs, concerns and situations encountered by the hospitalized and shut-in. Many of the prayers listed below can be easily adapted to correspond with various faith traditions.

> *"A powerful effect of prayer is the change it produces in the pray-er."*

A Prayer for God's Providence

Oh Lord, while it would be easy to surrender to doubt and fear, I choose to trust in your love. My confidence does not rest on any ability which I have to manage life. Although I am frail and my frame is dust, I am convinced that no situation is totally removed from your purpose.

Your faithfulness energizes me when my resources become exhausted, enabling me to find new possibilities in the most unlikely places. My days are often clouded by destructive forces, but I remain persuaded that eventually such forces will give way to the purpose of divine love.

My Lord, your constant care in days past assures me that I can trust myself to your love in days yet to come. Your providence assures me that the blackest night may usher in the brightest morning.

I do not know what the future holds, but I believe that you will remain close to me as I face it. So, dear Lord, as a child trusts in a loving parent, I entrust myself to you this day and all my days.

Amen

A Prayer for God's Help

Oh God, life is more than I can manage in my strength; I humbly bow in prayer. Sometimes, I confess, it is hard to pray. Deliver me from those who tell me my prayers are ineffectual because my faith is too small or your promises cannot be trusted. I am quite aware that I continually try to achieve spiritual goals by earthly means. Dear Lord, the world is still too much with me!

Ultimately, dear God, help must come from you. It is only as you free me from all confidence in human resources that I will be able to rely on you with child-like trust.

Help me to pray as I ought rather than as I want, to seek after increased compassion rather than self-serving advantage, to pursue after a strong spirit rather than an easy solution.

Your help will establish me in your mercies and affirm me by your peace. Enable me to learn something this day that will make me wiser and more at home with my destiny when day draws to its close. This I pray in whom I have both my beginning and my end.

Amen

A Prayer for Endurance

Dear God, your presence continually undergirds my life. Your love unfailingly reaches to the hidden corners of my heart. Remembering your steadfastness braces me for living today.

Strengthen me to endure the times when I cannot see the well-lighted path. Grant me the confidence that the shadow of trouble will fade in the sunlight of your presence. Create in me an endurance that goes beyond my capacities. Help me to stand upon the rock of your promises rather than upon the quicksand of my strength.

I celebrate your companionship which shortens long hours. My gratitude overflows because of your love which brings meaning and purpose even to suffering. Thank you for sharing the burdens that I cannot bear alone and for endurance which is your gift and not my achievement.

Amen

A Prayer of Thanksgiving for Hospitals

O God, I thank you that there are such places as hospitals, infirmaries and nursing homes. I thank you for those who have the skill to find out what is wrong and to put it right again. I thank you for those who, throughout the day and night, attend to those in discomfort, distress, and pain. I thank you that there are places where the ill, the weak and the old are not looked on as a nuisance, but where they find loving care and attention. I thank you not only for doctors and surgeons and nurses, but for all the people who do the many jobs which have to be done, if the work of the hospital is to go on – technicians, dispensers, dieticians, social service workers, nurses' aides, orderlies, secretaries, typists, clerks, porters, ambulance drivers, cooks, and kitchen maids. Help me to remember   all those who are helping you to make me well again, and to give thanks for them.

Amen.

A Prayer for the Medical Professionals and Support Staff

O God, I ask you to bless all those who care for me in this hospital. Bless the surgeons and the physicians. I thank you for the knowledge and for the skill which you have given to them. Bless the nurses. I thank you for their cheerfulness, their patience and their watchfulness all through the day and night. Bless those who cook the meals, those who clean the wards, and those who carry out the endless administrative duties that a place like this needs. Give to all who care for the sick, not only here but in all hospitals, infirmaries and nursing homes, joy and satisfaction in their work. And when they get tired of their work and a bit fed up with people like me, help them to remember how great a thing it is to ease the pains and heal the bodies of suffering men and women.

Amen.

A Prayer Before Entering the Hospital

O God, my Father, now that I know that I must go into the hospital, help me not to worry. Help me realize that worry only makes things worse, and that the more I worry the longer I will take to get better. Teach me that I am just as near you in a hospital bed as in my own home. Give me that peace of mind without which I know that I cannot have health of body.

Amen.

A Prayer After Entering the Hospital

O God, everything is new and strange and rather frightening. Half the time I don't know what is going on. Help me be serene, calm and relaxed. Keep me cheerful, and help me be a comrade to those who are feeling just as strange and just as afraid as I am. Help me not grumble or complain. Help me not be fussy and demanding. Help me be grateful for all that is done for me. Help me make the work of those who are looking after me as easy as I can. Help me forget my own troubles in doing something to help and cheer those who are worse off than I am.

Amen.

A Prayer for Hope

Eternal God, Father of us all, I come to thee in quietness and confidence. I thank thee for the gift of life and the strength of faith: faith which bears me up at all times; faith that sustains me in the strength of the everlasting arms. Support me through these days and make me whole again. Strengthen all those who serve thee through the healing ministries: doctors, nurses and all who serve the healing forces. Support my loved ones and strengthen them through faith.

Amen.

A Prayer for Strength

I pray to you, God, as the very heart of life, breaking, hurting, suffering with us. For how else would you understand my struggle if you did not hurt with us?

I pray that I may see you as gentle strength and seek to understand how you are also the laughter which mends the brokenness, the soothing peace after a long cry, the vision of hope which appears after the tears wash away.

I pray that I may see you as one who has chosen me. Give me new life, new laughter, new awareness of the beauty of life. Raise me up as an image of hope to the despairing and bringer of softness to a world hardened by pain.

O God, I pray to you as the very heart of life, beating your rhythm of healing within me.

Amen

A Prayer for God's Loving Presence

O God, I open my heart to you in this time of sickness and time of confusion, a time full of both fear and hope, questions and thanksgiving.

I pray that I may feel your healing power in this moment. May I feel this power as close to me as the air I breathe, as the blood running through my veins, as the hands that hold me in this moment. May I know that in moments such as this you, O God, suffer with me and guide me, always working for the mending of what is broken.

I pray that I may feel the love of family and friends who remember me in prayer, that I may feel this love as a warm comforting light holding me in the gentleness of grace.

Guide and keep me now that I might not lose sight of your love.

Amen.

A Prayer When Illness Is Minor

O God, in times like this when the normal routine of life is broken, I pray for a special sense of your presence. Though what I face does not carry great threat or deep danger, this is a moment of some fear and apprehension. I pray for calm and understanding, for the power of healing, and a vision of good recovery. Let me use this time of rest for good purpose and then return to the tasks that lie ahead with new strength and care.

Amen.

A Prayer in a Time of Confusion

God, I am a mixture here indeed. I hope; I doubt. I rise; I fall. I fidget; I fuss. Then, I experience a rising from some mysterious place. I hear you call my name. I turn and listen in faith. I pray now for the calming touch of grace, the blessing of peace. I pray that I may hear the word you have for me in this moment.

Amen.

A Prayer in a Time of Anxiety

There are times, O God, when it seems that the chain of life which held me together is broken, and I feel myself being hurled through a place of darkness and despair.

In this moment, I pray for your everlasting arms to catch and hold me, for angels to send help in the night, for light to break the darkness and grant me comfort and rest. Open my eyes that I may see such visions; open my heart that I may receive such love. Relax my tightened body that I may find the comfort of the everlasting arms.

I pray especially that I may feel that chain of life connected again, linking friends and families, faith and future, hope and love in a golden circle.

Give me grace in times of need, to give and receive your love which flows like an everlasting stream.

Amen.

A Prayer When Human Help Fails

O God, I think that everyone has done all that can be done, and I have the feeling that it is not enough. So I'm coming to you now because I have nowhere else to go. Make me quite sure that, whatever happens, nothing can separate me from you and that, whether I get better or not, I am in your hands. Help me not to be afraid anymore and not to worry anymore. I'm not giving in; I'll still hold on to life and do everything to get well. But make me sure that, whether I live or die, you are with me always, to the end – and beyond the end.

Amen.

A Prayer Before an Operation

O God, help me to remember at this moment that I have a very great deal for which to be thankful. I am grateful for the wisdom of the physician, the skill of the surgeon, the art of the anesthetist, and the kindness of the nurses. I am grateful for the merciful oblivion which anesthetics bring. Help me to be calm and relaxed, trusting the surgeon's skill, and trusting you. And make quite sure that, whatever happens, nothing can separate me from your love.

Amen.

A Prayer After an Operation

O God, operations are all in the day's work for the surgeon, the anesthetist and the nurse; but for people like me they are strange and alarming. I am so glad that I am through my operation, and that I am still alive! I can say that to you, knowing that you'll understand. I know that this is only the first step on the way back to health. Help me from now on to be a good patient, thankful and uncomplaining, always helping, never hindering those who are trying to make me well.

Amen.

A Prayer for the Critically Ill

O God, they don't need to tell me that it is going to be touch and go with me. I know quite well that I've got to be ready for anything. I know that the doctors and the nurses will do their very best for me. Give me the will to win through. Give me patience to bear my weakness, courage to endure my pain, obedience to accept whatever is best for me. If I am not going to get better, make me quite sure that, whether I live or die, nothing can separate me from your love. I think that I have got past the stage of worrying, but I know how anxious those who love me are. Bless them and help them not to worry but to leave everything to you. That is what I am doing.

Amen.

A Prayer When Healing Is Delayed

O God, I know that recovery cannot be quick. I know that the body takes its own time to heal. But I know that everything possible is being done for me. All the same, I get impatient. I want to be on my feet; I want to get home again; I want to get back to my work. O God, teach me what I know already. Teach me that the more impatient I am, the more I delay my recovery. Help me to learn to wait cheerfully, hopefully, uncomplainingly, and content to live one day and to take one step at a time.

Amen.

A Prayer for the Helpless and Bedridden

O God, even when I am lying here like this in bed, help me to count my blessings. I can still talk, and use my hands quite a bit. I can still send my mind and my imagination where my body cannot go. I can still remember, and I can still pray. Help me not grumble, not complain, not whine. Keep me cheerful, and help me make things as easy as I can for the people who have to look after me and the people who come to see me. And when things get so bad that I do want to break down and break out, help me do it when there is no one there to see but you because I know you will understand. Even on this bed, give me the joy that nothing and no one can take from me.

Amen.

A Prayer for the Puzzled and Perplexed

O God, sometimes I can't help wondering why this should have happened to me. You get a lot of time to think when you are lying in a hospital bed, and you see a lot of things in a hospital. Sometimes I cannot help wondering why there is so much suffering and pain in the world. I know that there just is not any answer to these questions, at least just now. So help me accept what I cannot understand. And help me be sure that this is not the only world, and that there is some place where the broken things are mended, where the lost things are found, where all the questions are answered, where all the problems are solved, where we know, even as we are known. So, in this world help me leave it all to you, in the certainty that I will never be tried beyond what I will be able to bear.

Amen.

A Prayer for One Injured by Accident

O God, I never thought when I went out that morning that I would end up here in this hospital. Now, I really know that life is an uncertain business, and that you never know what is going to happen. I do not really know whether the whole thing was my fault, or whether someone else was to blame. Do not let me start wondering about that. Just let me accept this, and do everything I can to help my own progress. Help those who love me to get over the shock that this must have been to them. Help them not to worry, but to be sure that I'm in good hands here. And when I get out of here, help me remember to be a lot more careful so that I will not get involved in an accident. I also pray that I will not be the cause of an accident to anyone else. I am very grateful that I am still alive and that things are no worse than they are. Help me be a good patient so that I will soon be on my feet again.

Amen.

A Prayer for One After Returning Home

O God, from this illness of mine I have learned one thing anyway – that you have got to lose a thing for a time in order to value it when you get it back. I never really appreciated my home until now. It's lovely to be back home; it's lovely to see and touch the old familiar things, and to be again with the people I love. Help me avoid two things. Help me avoid trying to do too much in order to show how well I am and undoing all the good that has been done for me in the hospital. And help me avoid acting the invalid and expecting to be waited on hand and foot. Give me a grateful heart and a sensible mind, and help me make steady progress until I am a hundred percent fit again.

Amen.

A Prayer for Family and Friends

O God, I think that just about the worst thing about this is being separated from my family and my home. Keep my family from worrying too much about me and from missing me too much. Help me realize that things will go on, even if I am not there, and that it is not for all that long anyway. Thank you for giving me good neighbors, good friends, good relatives to look after things and to help when I am not there. Help me remember that the more I worry about them, the slower will be my recovery and the longer I will take to get back to them. Help me lie back and relax for as long as I need with the certainty that, although I am separated from them, you are still with them and me.

Amen.

A Prayer for Other Patients

O God, keep me from praying to you as if there was no one in this hospital except me. Help me remember that I am only one person and one voice in this hospital, and in a world in which there are so many people in trouble. Bless every patient in this hospital: anyone who is lonely or frightened, anyone who is shy and nervous, anyone who is suffering a lot of pain, anyone who is making slow progress and who is discouraged, anyone who has had a setback today and who is disappointed, anyone who is worried and anxious, anyone for whom there is no recovery. Help me help others, and so forget my own troubles by sharing the troubles of others.

Amen.

A Prayer When Awaiting the Birth of a Child

O God, the months of waiting are ended, and my time is almost here. Take away all tension and fear, and make me relaxed and unafraid. Strengthen me for my ordeal, and give me joy in remembering that through me you are sending another life into this world.

Amen.

A Prayer After the Birth of a Child

O God, thank you for bringing my baby and me safely through everything. Bless my baby. Keep him/her safe from all the dangers of childhood. Bring him/her in safety to manhood/womanhood. Grant that some day he/she may do a good work in the world. Bless me. You have given me this great privilege; help me now be true to my great responsibility and never fail in the trust you have given to me. Help me when I get home again to make my home a place where you are an unseen but an always remembered guest.

Amen.

A Prayer at a Day's Beginning

O God, help me all through today. Help me to be grateful for any progress, however little. Help me not be discouraged by any setbacks, however disappointing. Help me be easy to help so that the doctors and nurses may find me to be a good patient. Help me help others who are also going through difficult times by being cheerful and sympathetic. Make me a good listener, more ready to listen to other people's troubles than to talk about my own. So, help me live through today in such a way that at evening I will have nothing to regret.

Amen.

A Prayer at a Day's Conclusion

O God, thank you for all that has been done for me today. Thank you for the people who looked after my body and my meals. Thank you for the people who thought out the treatment that I need and for all the people who gave it to me. Thank you for the people whose minds took thought for me and whose hands cared for me. Forgive me if at any time today I have been cross and impatient, unreasonable or uncooperative. Forgive me if I did anything to make the work of others harder and my own recovery slower. Help me now to sleep well and awaken refreshed tomorrow.

Amen.

Material in this section was adapted from several sources: *Hospital Handbook* by Lawrence Reimer and James Wagner; *Prayers for Help and Healing* by William Barclay; *How to Make Pastoral Calls* by Russell L. Dicks; and "Scriptural References and Prayers" from Baylor University Medical Center Chaplaincy Service.

Prayers of Various Faith Traditions

These selected prayers of differing religious traditions can be used in ministry to the patient and/or family of the patient during illness, dying, or at death. The list of faith traditions cited in this and other sections of this resource manual is not intended to be exhaustive, but merely representative of the plethora of various traditions.

Buddhist
Prayer for a Dying Person

Buddham Saranam Gaccami
I take refuge in the Buddha.
Dhamman Saranam Gaccami
I take refuge in the Dharma.
Sangham Saranam Gaccami
I take refuge in the Sangha.

And now I betake myself, Lord, to the Blessed One as my refuge, to the Truth, and to the Order. May the Blessed One except me as a disciple, as one who, from this day forth, as long as life endures, has taken refuge in them.

Prayer for the Deceased

Studying the same doctrine, under one master, You and I are friends.
See yonder white mists floating in the air on the way back to the peaks.
This parting may be our last meeting in this life. Not just in a dream,
but in our deep thought, let us meet often hereafter.

Christian (Catholic)

Prayer for the Sick

Let us pray now, asking God to help and to heal _____ and all who are suffering.

    May God bless _____ in this time of sickness, we pray:
        All: Lord, hear our prayer.
    May God comfort _____ family and give them peace, we pray:
        All: Lord, hear our prayer.
    May God help us to trust in his healing power, we pray:
        All: Lord, hear our prayer.
    May God guide all doctors and nurses in their work of healing, we pray:
        All: Lord, hear our prayer.
    May God heal all who are sick in body, mind, or spirit, we pray:
        All: Lord, hear our prayer.

Lord Jesus, we trust in your power to heal and to save, for you are the Lord of life both now and forever.
        All: Amen.

Prayer for the Dying

Go forth, Christian soul, from this world in the name of God the almighty Father, who created you in the name of Jesus Christ, Son of the living God, who suffered for you, in the name of the Holy Spirit, who was poured out upon you, go forth, faithful Christian. May you live in peace this day, may your home be with God in Zion, with Mary, the virgin Mother of God, with Joseph, and all the angels and saints.
        Amen.

Prayer for the Deceased

Eternal rest grant unto _____, O Lord and let perpetual light shine upon _____. May _____ soul and all the souls of the faithful departed through the Mercy of God rest in peace.
        Amen.

Christian (Protestant)

Prayer for the Sick

O Father of mercies and God of all comfort, our only help in time of need. We humbly beseech thee to behold, visit, and relieve thy sick servant _____ for whom our prayers are desired. Look upon _____ with the eyes of thy mercy; comfort _____ with a sense of thy goodness; preserve _____ from the temptations of the enemy; and give _____ patience under his affliction. In thy good time restore _____ to health, and enable _____ to lead the residue of life in thy fear, and to thy glory; and grant that finally _____ may dwell with thee in life everlasting through Jesus Christ our Lord.
Amen.

Prayer for the Dying

Almighty God, look upon this your servant, lying in great weakness, and comfort _____ with the promise of life everlasting, given in the resurrection of your Son Jesus Christ our Lord.
Amen.

Prayer for the Deceased

Depart, O Christian soul, out of this world in the Name of God the Father Almighty who created you, in the Name of Jesus Christ who redeemed you, in the Name of the Holy Spirit who sanctifies you. May your rest be this day in peace, and your dwelling place in the Paradise of God.
Amen.

Hindu

Prayer for the Sick

There is peace in the heavenly region; there is peace in the atmosphere. Peace reigns on earth. There is peace in water; medicinal herbs bring peace; there is peace in the vegetable kingdom; there is harmony in the celestial objects and peace in the eternal one. There is peace in everything; peace pervades everywhere. May that peace come to _____! May there be peace, peace, peace!

> Amen.

Prayer for the Dying

The door of the True is covered with a golden disk. Open it O Pushan, that we may see the nature of the True. O Pushan, only seer, O Yama (judge), O Surya (sun), son of Pfauapati, spread your rays and gather them! I see the light which is your fairest for I myself am He!

My breath to the air, to the immortal! My body ends in ashes. Om! Mind remember! Remember your deeds!

Agni, Lead us on to prosperity by a good path. O God, you know all things! Keep crooked evil far from us, and we shall offer you the fullest praise!

Prayer for the Deceased

> Asato maa sadgamaya
> Tamaso maa jyotirgamaya
> Mrityormaa Amritam gamaya

Lead me from untruth to truth; lead me from darkness unto light; lead me from death unto immortality.

Islamic

Prayer for the Sick

O Allah! The Sustainer of mankind! Remove the illness, cure the disease. You are the One who cures. There is no cure except Your cure. Grant (us) a cure that leaves no illness.

Prayer for the Dying

My Lord how can I despair of thy good regard for me after death, when in my life-time Thy treatment of me has been nothing but beautiful?

Cause us at the hour of death to repeat the *shahada* knowing what it is that we say. And be compassionate to us with the compassion of the lover to his loved one.

Give us the happy ending that You didst give to Thy saints, and make the best of our days the day when we shall meet Thee.

Have a good confidence in God that He will generously grant you a good ending, and that He will ease for you the pangs of death and the constriction of the grave.

The Prophet said: "Verily none of you shall die except confident in God the Most High." And he went to see a man in his death agony and said to him, "How do you find yourself?" He replied, "I find myself in fear of my sins and in hope of the mercy of my Lord." Then the Prophet said, "These two are never united in the heart of a servant in this world without God giving him what he hoped for and securing him against what he feared."

Jewish

Prayers for the Sick

May the source of strength who blessed the ones before us, help us find the courage to make our lives a blessing, and let us say, Amen.

Bless those in need of healing with *r'fua sh'leima*, the renewal of body, the renewal of spirit, and let us say, Amen.

Prayers for the Deceased

Hear O Israel, the Lord is our G-d, the Lord is One. (In a whisper, recite the following.) May His name of glory and majesty be blessed forever. You shall love the Lord your G-d with all your heart, with all your soul, and in all your ways. These words that I am commanding you today shall be in your heart. You should teach them to your children, speak them while returning home, while traveling on your way, and while dwelling in your place. You shall tie them as a sign upon your hand, and as frontlets between your eyes. You should write them upon the doorposts of your houses and gates.

The Lord is my Shepherd; I shall not want. He maketh me to lie down in green pastures; He leadeth me beside the still waters. He restoreth my soul; He leadeth me in the paths of righteousness for His name's sake. Yea, though I walk through the valley of the shadow of death, I will fear no evil; for thou art with me. Thou preparest a table before me in the presence of mine enemies; Thou anointest my head with oil; my cup runneth over. Surely goodness and mercy shall follow me all the days of my life; and I shall dwell in the house of the Lord forever.

(Important note on the prayer beginning with "The Lord is my Shepherd:" In the Christian tradition, Psalm 23 is used in ministry to people in many life situations – difficulty, illness, death, etc.. In ministry to people of the Jewish tradition, however, Psalm 23 is a prayer, among others, to be recited following one's death. Therefore, it would be ill-advised to offer this prayer to Jewish people who are sick, because they would believe that the sickness was unto death.)

Native American

Prayers for the Sick and/or Dying

O Great Spirit, Spirit Keepers of All the Directions; North, East, South and West; Grandfather Sky and Mother Earth, hear me. O Spirit Keepers of this place, hear me. O Spirit Guides of this One for whom we pray for now... (say the name) hear me. Hear our prayers, O Grandfather. Hear the prayers in the hearts of all his/her loved ones. O Grandfather, hear the prayers in this one's heart.

O Great Spirit, All My Relations, we give thanks for all things made whole and for the beauty of all that is as when first born. We hold in our hearts this One in the Light of Spirit, as when fresh and new, whole and healthy as when first born. We ask, O Grandfather, your blessing upon (name)'s spirit so that he/she may be refreshed in the Goodness and Beauty of Your Light. Bless (name) Great Spirit. Bless (name) O Spirit Keepers of the North. Bless (name) O Spirit Keepers of the East. Bless (name) O Spirit Keepers of the South. Bless (name) O Spirit Keepers of the West. Grandfather Sky, Bless (name). Mother Earth, Bless (name). All My Relations, Bless (name). We give thanks to you, All My Relations, All Spirit Keepers, Guides and Allies and to You, Great Spirit for Your blessings for (name). It is therefore in this moment we pray:

> Beauty before me, Beauty behind me.
> Beauty to the left of me and Beauty to the right of me.
> Beauty above me and Beauty below me.
> I walk in Beauty, In Beauty I walk.
>
> Spirit before you, Spirit behind you,
> Spirit to the left of you and Spirit to the right of you.
> Spirit above you and Spirit below you.
> You walk in Spirit, In Spirit, you walk.
>
> Beauty before us, Beauty behind us.
> Beauty to the left of us and Beauty to the right of us.
> Beauty above us and Beauty below us.
> We walk in Beauty, In Beauty, we walk.

Prayers for the Deceased

Naked you came from Earth the Mother. Naked you return to her.
May a good wind be your road.

Let go of the present and death.
Go to the place nearest the stars, gather twigs, logs;
Build a small fire, a huge angry fire.

Gather nature's skin, wet it, stretch it,
Make a hard drum, fill it with water to muffle the sound

Gather dry leaves, herbs, feed the fire.
Let the smoke rise up to the sky,
To the roundness of the sun.

Moisten your lips, loosen your tongue,
Let the chant echo from desert, to valley, to peak –
Wherever your home may be.

Remember the smoke, the chants, the drums,
The stick grandfather held as he spoke in the dark
Of the power of his father?

Gather your memories into a basket, into a pot,
Into your cornhusk bag, and
Grandfather is alive for us to see once again.

Some may say that the ways of the Old Ones are forgotten.
Many believe that they're gone.
I know, in your heart, if you keep the fire
The Old Ones will come back to you.

Just sing to the Mother, and She will come,
Sing to the Mother and She will come
Sing to the Mother and She will come,
O heyana, hene yo we.

When the ones you have loved have left you forsaken
And you cry to the winds all alone,
Reach into your heart and pull out your fire,
The One who will answer your call.

Then sing to the mother, and She will come,
Sing to your Mother, and She will come.
Sing to your Mother, and She will come,
O heyana, hene yo we.

Know that it's hard to be your own hero,
To rescue yourself from the fire.
The way through your heart is the one you must travel,
But, you don't have to do it alone.

Just sing to the Mother, and She will come,
Sing to your Mother, and She will come.
Sing to your Mother, and She will come,
O heyana, hene yo we.

Unitarian Universalist

Prayer for the Sick

Almighty God, help us to offer a prayer that is worthy of us, that we may think of those things that are most helpful to others as well as to ourselves. We pray for strength and better health for those who are ill. We pray for comfort and happiness for those whose minds and hearts have been saddened by loss. We pray for all persons who find meaning in the alleviation of suffering and fulfillment in the search for ways to overcome illness.

Prayer for the Deceased

O Thou, Who art the only Real and whose motion in our hearts is our truest self, we turn to Thee in perfect faith and in perfect trust. Our lives are bathed in mystery and touched by Thee in ways beyond our reach; we look not for explanations and we do not seek reasons for that which is not ours to explain. We come from Thee, we live in Thee, and we return to Thee; nothing harmful shall come to us, if we are children of the spirit, but all things shall work together for good.

Though grievous losses may befall, and though our hearts may burst, we know that birth and death are the lot of every being; we perceive that birth and death, frame differences in duration and felicity which are not of Thy kingdom. The only harm which can come to us is through the death of goodness in our hearts. Our faith is unshakable that if we trust and serve Thy Light we shall be led in paths of healing and of meaning beyond our power to see or understand.

We who come and go, in the long succession of the frail, we who walk in the procession of the ages, thank Thee and bless Thee for Thy nearness. We know that the final destiny of each and all, is mercifully of Thy making.

I sincerely hope that the prayers provided in this section will serve the purpose of broadening the effective scope of your ministry to the sick, dying, deceased, and their families during any of these stated times of crisis.

* Materials in this section were derived from a variety of sources: *Circle of Healing: Daily Prayers for Patients, Family and Friends; The Book of Common Prayer;* Midwest Bioethics Center's "Compassion Sabbath Resource Kit;" *Communion of the Sick; Pastoral Care of the Sick: Rites of Anointing and Viaticum;* "Emergency Ministry: Information and Resource for Clergy;" *Prayers; Prayer Thoughts.* Suggestions were also submitted by Sister Marsha Wilson on Catholicism, Rabbi Nathan Goldberg on Judaism, Rev. Kara Hawkins on Native American Spirituality, Anand Bhattacharyya on Hinduism, A. Rauf Mir, M.D. on Islam, Lama Chuck Stanford on Buddhism, and Rev. David A. Johnson and Vern Barnet, D. Min. on Unitarian Universalism.

Concluding Thoughts

Relationships and Illness:
A Paradox

"Leave me alone!" "Get out of here!" "You don't know how I feel!" Many of us have heard these and other similar comments from people who are experiencing physical pain. However, these sentiments reflect pain of a different kind: emotional and/or spiritual. While on the surface these words convey the message "I want to be alone" or "I am alone in my situation," they, on the other hand, may be a way that patients call out for help, companionship, someone to join them in their journeys of pain and frustration. These same patients may be surrounded by people – family, friends, church members – and yet feel alone because of the unwillingness or uncomfortableness of those people to enter that very different, frightening world of illness. Unfortunately, that happens all too frequently. Conversely, there are patients who intentionally push people away who are willing to enter their world because they (the patients) have not accepted their "lots in life."

How important to the healing process is acceptance?

> *"To accept our circumstances is another miraculous cure. For anything to change, or anyone to change, we must first accept ourselves, others, and the circumstances exactly as they are...."*

Acceptance of <u>self</u>, <u>others</u>, and the <u>situation</u> are essential criteria for living a full life in the midst of illness. The following statements are confirmation of this all-important principle:

❖ When I am ready to acknowledge the reality of the future of my illness, I will begin the process of an open and honest discussion with my family. (*Others*)

❖ I will search for meaning and purpose in my life each day in spite of the circumstances. (*Situation*)

- Each time I am tempted to ask "Why?", I will change the question to "what next?" or "How am I going to respond now?" (*Self*)

- I will try to sense God's presence in spite of what I hear from the medical reports, knowing that I am connected to God no matter what the situation. (*Situation*)

- When the circumstances seem to be overwhelming, I will know I have a choice in how I am going to respond. I will not blame my illness or other people for how I feel inside. (*Self*)

- I will try to see the impermanence of things as a sign of freedom. If I know all things change, I can let go and not have to grasp them so tightly. (*Self*)

- I will not stay preoccupied with my body or my illness. I will recognize that my body is not my total self but only part of it. (*Self*)

- As I seek relief from pain through medical solutions, may I also find relief from suffering through the healing of my emotions and spirit. (*Situation*)

Even though I have classified each of these maxims under one of the three categories of acceptance previously stated, in reality there is more of a convergence of these concepts rather than a rigid distinction.

This acceptance we are talking about can also be understood as "letting go," and such is masterfully articulated in a poem by Hank Dunn:

Giving Up and Letting Go

Giving up implies a struggle--
Letting go implies a partnership.

Giving up dreads the future--
Letting go looks forward to the future.

Giving up lives out of fear--
Letting go lives out of grace and trust.

Giving up is a defeat--
Letting go is a victory.

Giving up is unwillingly yielding control to forces
beyond myself--
Letting go is choosing to yield to forces beyond myself.

Giving up believes that God is to be feared--
Letting go trusts in God to care for me

It is apparent from this poem that a key element in "letting go" is the importance of relationships. They are vital to the holistic healing process. I indicated in another section of this manual that illness or disease often causes one to engage in a "life review." Prominent in these life reviews are relationships: damaged, distant, hostile, indifferent. Reconciliation is a desperate need for patient and family or friend at this critical juncture in their respective lives. In order to facilitate restoration between estranged individuals, I recommend the following:

Five Things of Relationship Completion

1. I forgive you.

"When we forgive, we set a prisoner free and discover that the prisoner we set free is us."

2. You forgive me.

"Is there anyone from whom I need to ask forgiveness? Or, is there anyone I need to forgive? Today is a good day to begin this process."

3. Thank you.

"May my thoughts this day turn toward gratitude for friends, family, memories of good times, special gifts. Gratitude is one attitude that can sustain people through the most difficult of circumstances."

4. I love you.

"These are the most beautiful and meaningful of all words that can literally change the entire course of one's life. Nothing is more powerful than love. The heartfelt need of every human being is to love and be loved."

5. **Goodbye.**

> *"In terminal illnesses, this 'goodbye' is to everything in life. However, in many other types of illnesses, goodbye might refer to habits or activities that can no longer be a part of one's life. Willingly relinquishing such things can enhance the quality of relationships with loved ones who encourage us to do so for our own well-being."*

Relationships that are reconciled and brought to completion form the basis for a new beginning, a new dimension in healing. One key to living well, and even dying well, lies in expressing the essence of these five things in our daily interactions to people with whom we intimately relate.

As pastoral caregivers, may we be acutely aware of the power of healthy, strong relationships with God and people in the healing of mind, body, and spirit. The intent of this discussion was to provide you with some helpful tips for the **Ministry of Reconciliation**. I want to conclude with a list of "lessons for living out of suffering" from the pen of Hank Dunn:

- ❖ *I have learned to live my life with so much more gratitude.*

- ❖ *I have learned to not let a day go by when I haven't said all I want to say to my family and friends.*

- ❖ *I have learned that even in the darkest hour a sense of humor can bring light.*

- ❖ *I have learned I have a choice in how I respond to any set of circumstances.*

- ❖ *I have learned that I must practice "letting go" and living peacefully my whole life if I hope to come to the end of my days in the same manner.*

❖ *I have learned to sense the presence of God in the most difficult circumstances.*

❖ *I have learned that one day everything will be taken from me. Therefore, I must nurture the things that will last. I will give attention daily to my inward spiritual life and to the love I share with others.*

---

* The material in this section was adapted from selections from *Light in the Shadows: Meditations While Living with a Life-Threatening Illness* by Hank Dunn, *Dying Well: The Prospect for Growth at the End of Life* by Ira Byock, M.D. and commentary by the author.

"The role that the minister, priest, rabbi, or lay counselor from the patient's own congregation plays in promoting the healing of hospitalized people remains vital."

~Harold Koenig, M.D.

"To care is to be there."

~Author

Appendix

Suggested Resources for Further Reading

Adams, Barbara Means. *Prayers of Smoke.*

Ali, A. Yusaf, translator. *The Holy Qur'an.*

Al-Qaradawi, Yusaf. *The Lawful and the Prohibited in Islam.*

Barclay, William. *Prayers for Help and Healing.*

Benson, Herbert, M.D. *Timeless Healing.*

Buehrens, John A. and Forrest Church. *A Chosen Faith: An Introduction to Unitarian Universalism.*

Caine, Kenneth Winston and Kaufman, Brian Paul. *Prayer, Faith, and Healing.*

Carrier, Gaston Marcel. *Prayers.*

Clebsch, William A. and Jaeckle, Charles R. *Pastoral Care in Historical Perspective.*

Cousins, Norman. *Anatomy of an Illness.*

Cousins, Norman. *Head First.*

Dicks, Russell L. *How to Make Pastoral Calls: A Guide for the Layman.*

Dossey, Larry, M.D. *Healing Words.*

Dossey, Larry, M.D. *Prayer Is Good Medicine.*

Dunn, Hank. *Hard Choices for Loving People.*

Dunn, Hank. *Light in the Shadows: Meditations While Living with a Life-Threatening Illness.*

Galanti, Geri-Ann. *Caring for Patients From Different Cultures.*

Grantham, Rudolph E. *Lay Shepherding: A Guide for Visiting the Sick, the Aged, the Troubled and the Bereaved.*

Gray, John, Ph.D. *Mars and Venus Together Forever.*

Gray, John, Ph.D. *Men are From Mars, Women are From Venus.*

Gyatso, Geshe Kelsang. *A Short Teaching on the Medicine Buddha.*

Holst, Lawrence E., editor. *Hospital Ministry: The Role of the Chaplain Today.*

Ikeda, Daisaku. *Unlocking the Mysteries of Birth and Death: Buddhism in the Contemporary World.*

Ivey, Allen E., Ivey, Mary Bradford, and Gluckster, Norma B. *Basic Attending Skills.*

Koenig, Harold, M.D. *The Healing Power of Faith.*

Kushner, Rabbi Harold S. *When Bad Things Happen to Good People.*

Lipson, Juliene, Dibble, Suzanne L., Minarik, Pamela A., editors. *Culture and Nursing Care: A Pocket Guide.*

Mahathera, Narada. *Buddhism in a Nutshell.*

Marshall, George N. *The Challenge of a Liberal Faith.*

Matthews, Dale, M.D. *The Faith Factor.*

Maxwell, Katie. *Bedside Manners: A Practical Guide to Visiting the Sick.*

May, Rollo. *The Art of Counseling.*

Mendelsohn, Jack. *Being Liberal in an Illiberal Age: Why I Am a Unitarian Universalist.*

Nikhilananda, Swami. *Man in Search of Immortality: Testimonials from the Hindu Scriptures.*

Nikhilananda, Swami. *The Bhagavad Gita.*

Padwick, Constance E. *Muslim Devotions: A Study of Prayer-Manuals in Common Use.*

Pasqualoni, Bonnie. *The Art of Healing: A Tibetan Buddhist Perspective.*

Patch Adams, a movie starring Robin Williams highlighting the importance of humor in patient care.

Powers, William K. *Oglala Religion.*

Remen, Rachel Naomi, M.D. *Kitchen Table Wisdom.*

Richmond, Kent D., and Middleton, David L., *The Pastor and the Patient: A Practical Guidebook for Hospital Visitation.*

Rinpoche, Sogyal. *The Tibetan Book of Living and Dying.*

Satprakashanda, Swami. *The Goal and the Way: The Vedantic Approach to Life's Problems.*

Snelling, John. *The Buddhist Handbook.*

Stolzman, William, SJ. *How to Take Part in Lakota Ceremonies.*

Stone, Howard. *The Caring Church.*

Storer, Robert Arthur. *Prayer Thoughts.*

Switzer, David. *The Minister as Crisis Counselor.*

USA Hospital Christian Fellowship publication. *Hospital Visitation.*

Villasenor, David. *Tapestries in Sand, the Spirit of Indian Sandpainting.*

Vrajaprana, Pravrajika, editor. *Living Wisdom: Vedanta in the West.*

Weintraub, Smith, editor. *Healing of Soul, Healing of Body*; a compendium of essays by rabbis dealing with the use of psalms in healing.

Worthington, Everett L., Jr., editor. *Dimensions of Forgiveness.*

Ywahoo, Dhyani. *Voices of Our Ancestors.*